The Journey:

Unleashing the Power of

Business Integration

The Journey:

Unleashing the Power of

Business Integration

Claire Bloom

Keith Launchbury

Chapters

Acknowledgments

We would like to acknowledge the incredible foresight of APICS, the Premier Professional Association for Supply Chain Management, for their development of the Certification in Integrated Resource Management (CIRM) curriculum which allowed us to help our students understand what was truly required to make a business operate as a cohesive, efficient, effective and successful enterprise. Sadly, the certification program no longer exists.

We would also like to recognize Celebrity Cruise Lines which provided us such a lovely environment in which we could write this novel.

Introduction

"The Journey" is the story of the evolution of a company as it moves from chaos to order, and from dis-integration to integration.

The journey is a labor of love of process, in the belief that everything is a process and if you get the process right then good will follow.

It is a labor of love of integration and order, out of the belief that if you work together with a specific goal at the forefront of your efforts, then you can overcome any obstacles.

It is a labor of love of community, out of the belief that we are all in this together, and that unless we all work together to succeed, we will all fail together.

It is a labor of love of leadership, out of the belief that leadership can come from anyone, even the most unlikely individual, and that by accepting this we learn better leadership skills.

It is finally, and most importantly, a labor of love, period.

Chapter 1

"Mommy," Jenny Kim's 10-year-old daughter Su said as she looked up at her over the top of the cereal box on the table. "Could you please talk with me tonight about your work? Our teacher asked us to talk to three people in our family and find out what they do for work and then report back to the class."

"Of course," Jenny replied. "And you can ask your daddy and Uncle Jimmy too since he is going to be here for dinner!"

"No, I already got my other two people. I asked Nana and Auntie Wei Ling."

Nana, Jenny's mother, sold Tupperware and Wei Ling, Jenny's sister, was a flight attendant. "I guess you are exploring lots of options! What do you think you want to be when you grow up?" Jenny asked.

The little girl straightened up in her chair and replied "I'm going to run a company just like you do!" Su beamed with pride and confidence.

Jenny wished she had that same confidence as she looked at her agenda for the day ahead. She had already received more than 20 emails, three of which had required immediate responses, and she hadn't checked the daily shipments report for the previous Friday so she needed to do that. On the way to work she needed to follow up with the shipping department to make certain that the part she had sent over to them had gone out priority overnight to their newest potential customer.

She didn't remember her father working quite this hard. In fact, she remembered him as being very present with the family, but Jenny felt disconnected since taking the company over upon his death just 18 months before.

She had been with the company since her graduation from business school and had excelled in marketing and sales, but running a company, she discovered, was a very different thing.

Besides the normal crises that occurred during a given day, she knew that today she had to talk with marketing about the sales forecast and engineering about a new product concept. She had to speak with finance about the updated income and expenses report for the month, and production about the available capacity in case the forecast was particularly good. She would meet with human resources to see if they had any success recruiting a new janitor, and procurement to see if they had identified a new supplier for one of the components in their product. Once again she wondered how her father had done everything that she was doing.

Jenny's grandfather had started the Lightning Bolt Company forty years ago, making power transformers, and after twenty-two years of successful growth, he succumbed to a heart attack leaving the company to his son. Jenny's father had done an amazing job growing the company, and he was responsible for developing the "SmartMegaPower system" that was now the leading network traffic controller energy utilities used to control the efficient generation and distribution of electricity. Upon his death, Jenny had taken over, and while she loved her work, she wished that there were fewer days that made her just plain crazy. Most days she got home after 6:30, and every day but Monday she left home at 6 in the morning. Mondays she saw Su off to school and then made her 20-minute journey to work right behind the school bus.

Just then, Jenny's husband George came in, and kissing Su on the top of her head, and Jenny on the cheek, he cheerily asked, "What are my girls up to this morning?"

Su answered first. "Mommy and I are going to talk about her job tonight!"

"Really?" replied George. "You know that mommy's job is really hard! Are you sure you wouldn't rather talk to me? I have an easy job! All I do every day is talk to my plants."

George was a botanist and happily ran his own nursery where he dug in dirt, played with fertilizer, adjusted light and water, and managed to grow the most spectacular plants Jenny had ever seen. He generally left the management and administrative tasks to his assistant, Julie.

"No," Su answered. "I want to know about mommy's work." George smiled at Jenny, who shrugged her shoulders, and poured him coffee.

"I have something new for your office," George said as he handed her a box with a ribbon tied around it. "Give it to Lori," he added. "She will love it."

Lori was Jenny's Girl Friday, doing much of Jenny's administrative work including keeping her on track for her various meetings and maintaining communication with the various department heads. She was terminally cheerful, fervently positive, and perpetually helpful. She and George shared a love of all living plants, and they often talked about her garden and George's experiments with plant care.

Less than 15 minutes later, the three of them were out the door on the way to their respective activities little knowing that Jenny's work life and The Lightning Bolt Company were about to change dramatically.

Chapter 2

Jenny pulled into her parking space and viewed the sign that said "CEO" with a certain amount of pride accompanied by the same underlying panic that struck her every morning. Once again she acknowledged that she simply didn't feel confident that she could do the job. It didn't matter, however, the job was hers, so grabbing her briefcase and the box for Lori, she locked her car and walked in the front door.

She remembered when she was a child, walking in to visit her father and much later helping him design the new lobby, which now held a scale model of the "SmartMegaPower" system as well as photos of the production line. It also held Lori's desk.

As Jenny entered the building, Lori cheerfully asked, "How was your weekend?"

Lori's smile always raised Jenny's spirits, and she handed her the box saying, "George sent you another plant - at least I think that is what this is!"

Lori's smile turned to a full 100 watt grin as she gently took the box from Jenny and opened it.

"Oh my God!" she exclaimed. "How did he do this?"

She gently removed an exquisite apricot-colored flowering plant from the box, and turning to Jenny said, "These daisies are normally bright yellow, but he found a way to grow them in this lovely shade of orange!"

Jenny shrugged her shoulders. "You know George! He is always playing with the plant food and the lights.

"Tell him 'Thank You!'"

"Can you see if Dave is available to talk with me about that janitor position?"

"Sure," Lori replied, and Jenny walked into her office.

A minute later Lori poked her head in and said "Dave says he has a live one, and you should come down to talk with him about it."

"Tell him I am on my way but I have to stop by shipping first. I'll just be a few minutes."

"Ok," replied Lori, and Jenny left her office and turned down the hall leading to the functional areas of the company. At the shipping office she found Maya, who was in charge of distribution and customer service, talking with the Jim, the shipping supervisor.

"Maya, I'm glad to find you here. I wanted to check with you about the shipments for Friday. I didn't have a chance to check before everyone went home, but did we make the end of month shipment numbers?"

"We did," Maya responded, "but it wasn't the way we had planned. We had a last minute cancellation from the Magellan Nuclear Power Station. They have an inspection coming up and can't replace their controller right now, so they asked us to delay shipment for three weeks."

"I wish there was a way to coordinate these inspections and our shipments a little better," Jenny said. "This isn't the first time that we've had cancelled shipments at the last minute because of an inspection. Isn't there a schedule of these things?"

"Most of them are well known, but we have never asked about them. Perhaps Val can program the order entry system to prompt customer service to ask if there are any upcoming events that we need to program into the shipping date." Maya's idea was a good one, so Jenny made a mental note to talk to her head of IT about it.

"I'll talk to her," Jenny said. She turned to Jim. "Did that package get out to Sanborn Friday?"

"Yes, it went out," Jim replied, and Jenny took that task off her mental list.

"Thanks," she said, and turned to walk down to Dave's office.

Dave stood as she entered, and handed her an application. "I think we should take a look at this guy for the janitor job," he told Jenny.

Jenny sat in the chair across from his desk and read through the application. The applicant's name was Paul Jenkins, and he had just moved to the area from North Carolina, where he had held virtually the same position with a manufacturing company that Jenny was trying to fill. "Did you check his references?" she asked Dave.

"Yes, everything checks out," he replied.

"What brought him here," Jenny asked, "and how long will he stay?"

"He moved here with his wife, who works for one of the pharmaceutical companies in South San Francisco, and you know how they are. She will probably never leave, so I think he is a good bet," Dave responded.

"Ok! Another biggie off my list! When can he start?"

Dave replied, "He is ready to start tomorrow! He waited to apply until they had found a place to live and were all moved in."

"Terrific," Jenny exclaimed! Let's get him in at 7 tomorrow."

"Will do," replied Dave. "Have a great day!"

Jenny left feeling fairly positive as she continued on to the finance/IT office to talk with Val about the month end and the possible programming of the order entry report.

Finding out from Val that the programming would be fairly straightforward, and that the month end results were as expected (more money had come in than had gone out), Jenny returned to her office.

There she found Brian, her very impatient production supervisor, pacing, and as he saw her he started in immediately.

"Olga just told me that she just sold twenty more systems than we can make this month."

"Ok……………" Jenny said. "Can't we just put some folks on the weekends for the next three weeks?"

"Some of our people have vacation scheduled this month. I don't know if or how we can get the parts we would need, and one of our CNC machines is due for annual maintenance" he said, referring to the Computer Numerical Control machines. "I have no idea if I can make this happen," he moaned, and muttering to himself he walked out.

Jenny turned to Lori. "Please get Olga on the phone for me," she asked.

"You bet," Lori replied, and turned to dial the head of sales and marketing.

When Jenny got on the phone Olga sounded very excited. "Jenny, it is great news! Barkley Power and Light just decided to convert to the use of the "SmartMegaPower" system and ordered twenty units for immediate delivery!"

Jenny could totally understand Olga's enthusiasm. Having come from marketing and sales she knew how important it was to finally get the big order after working hard on the presentation and all of the requisite follow up with the customer. She was also, and not for the first time, having to run interference between the aggressive and successful marketing and sales department and production. It was transactions such as this one that made her think that she was not the right person for this job.

"Olga, that is great news, but Brian just came to me and said he isn't sure he can fill the order."

Olga complained "Brian is always complaining about not being able to make enough systems. With an order like this he should be jumping through hoops to get the work for his people. They will love the overtime, and we can hire a plane to bring in the parts and still make money. I don't know why he doesn't just see it like I do."

Jenny didn't want to discourage Olga's initiative in any way, but as usual it was her job to balance the competing demands of her two department heads, keep the company making money and keep customers happy. "I'll talk to him after he has had a chance to cool down," she said, but she wished that Olga and Brian would just work it out together and leave her out of it.

By the time she had responded to a few more problems, answered her emails, drafted a few letters, and reviewed the new marketing photos and brochures she realized that Lori was packing up and leaving for the day. She was hungry and realized she hadn't had any lunch, hadn't talked to Brian, and knew that George and Su would be expecting her home for dinner. Somehow the day had gotten away from her and she felt like she was further behind than when she had started.

She sent an email to Olga, Brian, and Val authorizing them to offer overtime to the production team, expedite ordering and shipment of parts, and she asked them to come to her with any problems or questions. She shut down her computer for the night wondering how she was going to explain to Su what she did for work without sounding negative and discouraged.

Chapter 3

Fortunately for Jenny, by the time dinner was over she was once more in her comfort zone, and as she talked with Su about her work she regained her sense of pride in what her family had accomplished in growing The Lightning Bolt Company.

"It isn't always fun managing people," she explained to her daughter. "They each have an idea about how things should be done, and they don't always talk to each other. My job is often to figure out what each of them wants, and then help them to see how they can help each other. It can be very satisfying when everyone suddenly sees how they can do more and help the customer more, but sometimes I feel like I am a referee."

"But you are the boss!" Su exclaimed. "Don't they have to do what you say?"

"Yes, sort of," Jenny replied. "But I have to be careful to make sure that they don't get angry with me! They are all important, and I need for them to keep on doing their best. If I make them angry, they might quit, and then where would I be?"

"Well, I would just tell them to grow up and get along!" Su said.

"That would be something to see," Jenny replied. "The important thing about being the boss is that really, you are there to help everyone else! You are the one who can make decisions that can make people's jobs easier, or harder, so you have to be careful."

"Maybe I will just be a Flight Attendant," Su said solemnly.

"Whatever you decide to be, you will be great!" Jenny reassured her daughter. "Now go get a good night's sleep so you can have a good day in school tomorrow!"

The next morning Jenny was in her office at 6 to find emails from Olga saying "Thank you," from Val saying she would do what she could and still keep the company in the black, and from Brian saying he would ask his people if they were willing to work the overtime. She replied with thanks to each of them, and by the time Lori had come in, she had requested a time to get together with Raj in research and development to see if he had any ideas on how they could expand their product line in a way that would contribute to the bottom line without stretching their capital outlay too far.

A few minutes after 7, Dave appeared in her doorway with a man beside him, and said, "Jenny, I'd like to introduce Paul Jenkins, our new Janitor."

16

Jenny was a bit surprised to see that Paul was older than she expected, probably in his mid-fifties, with short grey hair and a wiry thin body. She stood up and walked to the front of her desk with a smile on her face, and held out her right hand to shake Paul's hand.

"Paul, how nice it is to meet you. Dave, does Paul have time to chat before you show him around?"

"Sure," said Dave, and he turned to Paul. "Jenny will call me when she is ready to have you picked up, and then I will give you a tour."

"Thank you," said Paul, and as Jenny gestured to the chair in front of her desk, Paul stood in front of it, waited for her to sit down, and then sat down himself.

"Paul, I know that Dave will tell you all about how the company started, what we do, and how we have grown to where we are today, but I want to tell you a little bit about how we work, and what you will probably learn pretty quickly just by observing what happens around here.

"We are a small company, only about 100 people, and so everyone wears lots of hats, and does lots of different jobs. Some of us like the energy that comes from that and others would prefer to just do one job and come in and leave at the same time every day.

"Because of that you will find people here working odd hours, and that will make your job a bit more difficult. Mostly they are used to having someone work around them, so don't hesitate to do what you need to do even if there are people working. If you have to put off doing something because you just can't get to it, don't worry. There is always another day around here, but I would really like to see things spruced up a bit. If you have any recommendations for how we can do that, please don't hesitate to let me know how I can help.

"Is there anything you would like to tell me about how you usually work?"

Paul smiled, and said "That is very much the same as my last company. They made engines, and sometimes that was a very messy job, and often people worked late, but I made sure that everything got done in as timely a manner as I possibly could, and I enjoyed creating as attractive an environment as I could. It sounds like you are looking for the same thing here."

"Exactly," Jenny smiled. "As you are walking around with Dave, make notes about where you might be able to spruce things up and then let's meet again and talk about it next Monday. I usually get in every day but Monday at 6:00, but Monday I get my daughter off to school and am here at around 8:30."

"Sounds great, thank you," said Paul, and he stood to leave just as Lori stuck her nose in the office to say good morning.

"Lori, this is Paul Jenkins," Jenny said. "He is going to spruce up the place. Paul, this is Lori Kennedy. She runs me and pretty much runs the company."

Lori smiled, and held out her right hand to Paul.

"Hi, Paul," Lori said. "Feel free to come by and ask me if you need anything. I sit right out here, and guard the lion's den."

Jenny told Lori about Paul's appointment with her for the following Monday morning, and asked Lori to call Dave to come and take Paul on a tour.

"Thank you Paul. I know that this will work out well for both of us," Jenny smiled as Paul followed Lori out the door.

"I will see you on Monday," Paul replied, and Jenny was left to her work.

Chapter 4

As the remainder of the week went by, Paul had access to every area of the company, every room, every closet, every waste basket, and every desk. He saw printed reports in the trash, materials and supplies all over the place, perfectly good materials in the dumpster, and what looked to him like a lack of pride in the workplace evident nearly everywhere. What he saw really made him think, and when he compared it to where he had been working for the last 15 years, he thought that he might truly be able to make a difference.

After he and Jenny had greeted each other on the following Monday, he asked Jenny if he could paint the cafeteria walls.

"I think it would improve the light in there if I painted the walls white. Then I would like to paint a mural of some kind on one of the walls. If you don't like it, I can paint right over it, but I am a fairly good artist, and I think that it would brighten up the cafeteria and might make the lunch period a little more enjoyable for everyone. The paint and supplies would cost about $200."

Jenny thought it was a simple enough request, and authorized the expenditure. She was intrigued at what

Paul had in mind, and she realized that she herself didn't particularly like to eat in the cafeteria, and usually ate at her desk, not just to save time, but because the cafeteria was somewhat gloomy.

In the meantime Brian had gotten enough people to agree to work overtime to meet the demand of the additional twenty systems. He and Val had arranged for the expedited delivery of the parts, and Val and Olga had reported to Jenny that the profit margin would be quite a bit less than usual, but they agreed that by meeting the Barkley demand they had gained a new customer. They hoped that the Barkley demand would ultimately add significantly to the bottom line.

On Friday of Paul's second week, Lori came rushing into Jenny's office and said "Come quick! You have got to see this!"

Jenny followed Lori onto the shop floor, through the production area, and into the cafeteria, where she was blown away by how bright and cheerful it was. The walls were a crisp and clean off-white color. The chairs had all been painted a light blue and the tables had all been painted a slightly darker blue. The whole effect was light, airy, and professional. Jenny watched as people walked in for lunch, were struck silent, and then started exclaiming cheerfully to one another about the difference, and then sat down to eat with smiles on their faces.

There was no evidence of the mural that Paul had said he would paint, but if he did nothing more, Jenny was convinced that he had worked a miracle as she saw the people eating lunch chatting with one another in a way she had not seen before.

Jenny went back to her office, and paged Paul. When he arrived, she invited him to sit, and closed her office door.

"Paul," she said. "You have really done an outstanding job in the cafeteria. Everyone is talking about how much they love the new look. I'm very pleased with what you have done, and you certainly don't have to go to all the trouble of painting a mural. It looks great the way it is! Thank you!"

Paul's face reddened slightly, and he replied "Thank you for noticing. I will still do the mural, but it will take a little time. I am still gathering ideas about what to paint, but I promise, if you don't like it I will paint right over it."

Jenny smiled broadly, and thanked him again, saying how much she appreciated the hard work he had put in to making everyone so much happier with the cafeteria.

Things were looking up.

Chapter 5

Three weeks later on a Tuesday morning, when Jenny arrived at work at 6 am she found a note on her door that said: "Please meet me in the cafeteria at 9 am." The note was unsigned and she thought it must have something to do with the mural.

Just before 9 she went to the cafeteria, but instead of Paul, she saw her department heads sitting around a table in the middle of the cafeteria. "Which one of you called this meeting?" she asked.

No one replied.

"I assumed it was you, Jenny," Dave said.

"I didn't send this note," Jenny replied.

"Why on earth are we here?" Jenny asked. "Is someone playing games with us?"

"Why are we wasting our time? I have a lot of work to do," Olga demanded.

"You are the one who keeps causing problems, making promises we can't keep," Brian said angrily.

"Calm down, Brian," said Jenny.

"I don't have time for stupid meetings. I have work to do. I am leaving this nonsense," Brian stated.

"This is just typical. He always flies off the handle. No wonder we have such a hard time keeping good people in production," Olga offered.

"Stop it both of you," said Jenny. "This is not a presidential debate!"

Silence descended on the room as Olga and Brian exchanged angry glances.

On the table in front of them lay a single colored pencil.

Val picked it up and read the lettering. "This pencil says 'Organize Teams.' What does that mean?"

Dave said "Everyone knows what a team is. I played on a soccer team at school, and everyone in the team learned to play together. We learned the strengths and weaknesses of every player on our team so that we could improve our performance and win our matches."

Jenny said "Yes, that's obvious, but we are not playing soccer here so what does this have to do with us?"

Raj, normally the quiet one, softly said "Perhaps things would work better for us if we started behaving more like a team."

There was silence in the room.

Jenny finally replied slowly "Maybe this isn't a waste of time. Maybe this pencil is like a fortune cookie, telling us what direction we need to go to make our lives easier and our business more successful. I wonder what might happen if we all thought more like a team and less about our own individual responsibilities."

After a few moments Brian said "I grew up in a small village, and we all took care of each other. If one person was sick, everyone else would pitch in and help. If someone was in trouble there would always be someone in the village to offer help and guidance. We were never on our own. We had a sense of community."

Raj agreed. "When I came to America I was amazed at how isolated people were. Even those who live in big cities don't interact much with others. People go to work without talking to anyone. They do their work and then go home to their own families, and there is simply not the sense of community at work that I experienced in Goa."

Jenny said, "We all come from different backgrounds, different cultures and have different life experiences, so how can we bring all this to work for the good of the company?"

Val replied, "Why don't we start meeting like this for a few minutes every day? We can meet here in the cafeteria at 9 and talk about what each of us is doing that day, and talk about any problems or conflicts that come up and agree on a course of corrective action to solve each problem."

"That would sure make my life easier," Jenny said. "It seems that every time I meet with one of you I walk away with some action item that I have to take on with someone else. If we could organize ourselves as a team responsible for running this company together, then I we could just talk about it together instead of me running around talking with each of you about it separately." Jenny had the sudden sense that a heavy load was about to be lifted off her shoulders. "I will make all of you members of my executive team, and we will start meeting daily to review where we are and start working together as a team."

Maya had not said a word, but expressed her own feelings. "Wow, I am sure glad we got this invitation to meet here. It is like someone knew what we needed to do and planted a seed in our brains."

Olga said, "A good place for us to start might be how to handle another event like the Barkley order. I know we don't ever want to turn business away, and I know that it is my job to get us all the business I can, but it doesn't do us any good if Brian can't make the product."

Jenny agreed. "Let's see if we can work through this and make these unexpected orders a more positive experience. What are some ways we can make this happen?"

Dave agreed, but added "How can we prevent a great order from becoming a crisis?"

Jenny jumped in. "We shouldn't be thinking about how to stop customers from buying our products. We should figure out how to satisfy their needs in the most effective way possible. What do we need to be able to fill these unexpected orders?"

Brian knew that this question was directed at him, so he responded, "Well if we had extra parts and raw materials we could manage to produce those additional orders that exceed our forecast. We would need to be able to get extra people for the same reason."

Jenny asked, "How much more material, and how many extra people?"

"It would depend on the size of the order ," Brian said.

Jenny called on Olga. "Think about all the customers and potential customers you are talking with right now. What do you think is the biggest order you might get that you were not expecting?"

Brian added, "If you give me a number, I can get back to you by tomorrow with exact information on what I need to stock to meet unexpected demand."

Jenny replied, "That sounds like a good plan. Let's do it."

She turned to Val, who was still holding the pencil. "Can I have that?" she asked.

"Sure," Val replied, and handed the pencil to Jenny.

"Thanks everyone," Jenny said. "I would still like to know who decided that we needed to get together and talk about his, but it doesn't really matter now. What matters, is that we have learned how important it is for us to feel and act like a team, and to help each other when we get in a bind. Now let's all get back to work!"

With that, everyone stood up and moved back to their offices. Jenny looked once more around the cafeteria, smiled at the cheerful look, and walked back to her office. She actually felt relieved that she might not have to fix every problem in the company herself. She still wondered who had sent the notes, and who had left the pencil, but she acknowledged that it had brought them together and enabled them to think about the business in a different way.

She realized that she hadn't had the luxury of picking the people on her team. She knew that perhaps she might have chosen differently, making sure that she had the right blend of personalities and skill sets that were needed, and that their job descriptions included reaching out to the other departments regularly, but this was the team she inherited along with the Lightning Bolt Company. She knew that the hard feelings between Brian and Olga might continue, but she thought that if these meetings forced them to work together, they might learn from each other and find some common ground. The teamwork seed had been planted and Jenny would make sure that it had plenty of room to grow.

Chapter 6

Jenny's newly formed executive team began meeting daily in the Cafeteria at 9:00. Typically they would grab a beverage, sit around the table, and take turns talking about what was happening in their area.

It surprised Jenny to find out how many things they talked about impacted other members of the team, and they had frequent boisterous discussions about which of them might be interfering with the actions and the plans of the other. Each time, as tempers began to flare, one of the others would remind them that together they were just trying to keep the company moving in the right direction, keep the customers happy and loyal, keep people employed, keep growing, and keep doing the right thing.

As expected, the biggest arguments continued to be between Olga and Brian, but the conversation gradually moved from aggressive posturing, through informing each other and finally to actually checking with each other to ensure that their plans didn't conflict.

One day when they walked into their meeting Maya saw another pencil on their table. Her eyes flew wide open, as she looked at Val, and saw her eyes equally huge! Silence reigned, until Jenny walked in and said, "What's wrong?"

Silently, Olga, Val and the rest of the team looked down at the table. Jenny's glance followed their own, and her eyes reflected the same surprise as the others as she reached down and picked up the pencil.

"Identify Needs," was the message.

After a moment during which the pencil was passed around the table Jenny said "Well, right now I think I need to switch to decaf!"

Laughter ensued, breaking the tension in the group, and so Jenny continued. "Ok, let's just ask the question, what do each of you need?"

Brian started first.

"Well, to provide the safety cushion that we need to handle another big order like the one from Barkley, I need three more CNC machine operators and a night time maintenance worker so that the maintenance can be done off shift. Then I need about $120,000 in additional raw materials and parts. I also really need a more accurate sales forecast."

Jenny looked amused. "Interesting needs, Brian! As you all know after all the conversations we have had, we don't always know when the customers we are talking to will place an order, or how soon they will want our products, so perhaps we need to talk about what our absolute needs are, and what are wants, and what are dreams.

Raj asked "What is the difference between needs, wants, and dreams? Is it just a question of how essential they are, like Maslow said in his 'Hierarchy of Needs'?"

"What do you think?" asked Jenny.

"Well," Raj replied, "I agree that the most urgent needs are things critical to our survival, like air, water, food, shelter, and high speed Internet. Then there are wants, things that would be nice to have but they are not really necessary for our survival as a species. That would be things like Rolex watches, Cappuccinos, fine wines, and then there are things that we can only aspire to have, like world peace, social justice, winning the lottery, finding a perfect soul mate."

"Sounds good," Jenny chuckled, "but I am not sure high speed Internet is a need unless you are of an age where you were born with a mobile phone in your hand." She was thinking about how long Su could go without checking her mobile device, and figured the answer was probably measurable in milliseconds.

Olga was ready. "I need to have consistent and reliable delivery of products on a regular basis to my customers. I need to have the complete freedom to offer whatever is necessary to satisfy the customer. Even if a customer wants a product every day I need to be able to accommodate that. I want to see growth in sales revenue, and I want every customer order delivered on time, in full. I want to make sure that we satisfy every customer need, and most of their wants. That would make my dreams come true."

"Ok, let's make a note of that please, Lori." Jenny was glad she had asked Lori to join their meetings and record the discussions for future reference. Lori was dutifully compiling notes on her tablet.

"Thank you Olga, great start. Let's move on to Dave. What are your needs, wants and dreams?"

"I need money, I want to have a secure job and to contribute to the company and I dream about starting my own business. My wife is pregnant and I am the only breadwinner, so I am feeling a lot of responsibility on my shoulders."

Over the next few days they continued to discuss the ideas prompted by the latest pencil. They collected ideas, sorted them into needs, wants and dreams, and the discussion turned to the area of unmet needs. They realized together that every product that the company had ever developed was in response to an area where there was a need that was not being met.

Jenny was reminded of a story about a very creative ten-year-old Masai boy in Uganda who was upset when a lion killed the only bull they had. He developed a solar powered device to keep lions away from the cattle. When he had proven that it worked, he then made many of them and sold them to other families. The unmet need was something to keep lions away from cattle, and the solution was a solar powered device that flickered lights that frightened the lions.

Olga said, "If we specify our business needs correctly, then we should be able to satisfy our customers' requirements completely. The customers tell us exactly what they need, how many they need, when they need them, where they need them and how much they are willing to pay for them. We just have to figure out how to meet their requirements."

Dave said, "I understand that a requirement then includes the specific product, the specific quantity, the specific date by which they are needed, and the price that they will be paying."

Olga said, "Yes. The customers are very good at telling us exactly what they need, but they also have wants that they try to get at the same time for no additional charge. It is human nature to say that everything is a need, when in reality many things are

37

simply not essential but are just nice to have. I think that the difference is that the *need* to the customer is something they are prepared to pay for, and the *want* for them is something that would be nice to have, but that they are usually not willing to pay for."

Jenny decided to pursue her idea about expanding the product line, and when there was a lull in the conversation she raised the issue to the group.

"Raj and I have been talking about whether or not it might be time to expand our product offering. The "SmartMegaPower" system is doing very well in the commercial market, but we have been thinking about offering a product in the residential market. Raj, could you tell everyone what we are thinking?"

Raj, usually the quiet one, seemed a bit uncomfortable to be put on the spot, but he opened his notebook and started to talk about the idea of how the "SmartMegaPower" system might be scaled down to help residential customers better manage the power that they used in their homes.

"We can't ask our existing customers about this because they consider the new product a threat to their revenue. If consumers use electricity more wisely they don't need to buy as much energy. We also can't ask the consumers directly what they need because they have no experience of what is possible with a smart energy controller for home use.

Brian was furious! "When were you going to tell me about this? I am only the one responsible for making the product. I really should have been involved from the beginning!"

Olga added, "This product has the potential to be huge! It is a breakthrough product and could have a very high level of sales quickly, but I can't sell it with the same approach that worked with the energy utilities, so I need to hire someone with good social media and video presentation skills to create promotional videos, coordinate celebrity endorsements and directing the social media message."

Brian exclaimed, "You can market it all you want! If I can't make it there will be nothing to sell!"

Dave also had a comment. "You are going to have to hire a bunch of new people, and no one involved me either. My office can barely keep up with the benefits administration, hiring, training and payroll for the people we have. I will have to hire new people as well."

Val had her own concerns. "How do you think you are going to fund this start up anyway? We are doing well, but what kind of investment are you going to have to make, and what kind of return are you expecting?"

Maya, in charge of distribution and purchasing, was equally concerned and wasted no time in saying so. "With a new product line will come new distribution requirements, new parts and materials requirements, and new storage requirements. Tim, our facilities manager isn't even in this meeting, and he is going to have to work on factory layout, and everything else that will be needed to make this happen."

Everyone was furious, at Jenny and Raj.

Jenny interjected, "Brian, you are absolutely right. Raj and I should have talked with you about how we can add the capacity necessary to produce these devices once they have been proved effective. Olga, you are also right. One of the things that will need to be done is to develop a marketing plan for how to sell the idea to residential customers, with data from a pilot project and case studies with a savings calculator that shows the individual consumer exactly where savings can be realized.

"Maya, Dave, Val, you are all right, but you are acting as though we are going to be making this product tomorrow! Right now, this is just an idea! Let's table this for now, and think about what we each need if we decide to follow through with this idea, and talk about it more next week."

As they left, everyone seemed serious and thoughtful, and Jenny wondered whether the team could pull together and make this happen. She picked up the second pencil, thought about how she was being guided by an unseen hand, and wondered if teamwork ever really worked.

Chapter 7

The morning meetings were tense for the next few days, and Jenny contemplated cancelling them, but she realized that this would be a step backwards. They had grown a lot as a team, and once they got through this misunderstanding she thought that they would perform well again.

After a long weekend, she placed the second pencil on the table and said, "I don't want to raise a difficult subject again, but as we talk about how we identify needs. I want to ask if any of you have given serious thought to what your department would need if we decided to move forward with this project?"

No one wanted to be the first to speak, but Maya finally said, "I really think we need to bring Tim, our facilities manager, in on these meetings. So far there hasn't been a lot to talk about anything that would mean major changes to the facilities management area, but this will."

Jenny replied, "Maya, you are right. Lori, please call Tim and see if he can come down."

Lori stepped away from the table, and during her absence everyone was silent. On her return she reported that Tim would be right down, and they all quietly waited.

Tim arrived quickly, and humorously said, "So, this is the famous morning meeting! I wondered when you were going to invite me."

Jenny was on the spot to reply, and so she said, "Tim, I am sorry that you haven't been included but I am fixing that right now. Please come each morning at 9 and help us as we work together to try to make this company even more successful than it already is.

"About a week ago, Raj and I mentioned that we were talking about adding a new product to our offering. We hadn't gotten very far in the conversation when it was pointed out to us that each person here at the table has a vested interest in how that conversation progresses. I asked everyone to please consider what their actual needs might be if we decided to go through with developing a scaled down version of the "SmartMegaPower" system for the residential and small business market.

"As the person in charge of our facility, from the floor to the roof, your views certainly count, and so we all wanted you here."

Tim thought quietly, and asked, "Are you thinking of building another building, using our existing machines in our building, renting space, or buying another location?"

Raj answered, "We haven't even gotten that far. Right now we are just in the talking phase about whether or not it would even benefit us to start with a new product, much less how and where to make it."

"Well," Tim said. "Until you have that figured out there is little I can tell you except to say that as you are figuring it out, these are the kinds of questions you are going to have to answer. Once you have an idea of how much space you will need I can see if I can rearrange how we use our space now to get you that space, or find out options for other space that we don't own now."

"Thanks, Tim," said Jenny. I would really like you to sit in on our meetings so you can follow along through the whole conversation."

"Sure," said Tim. "I would be happy to," and he sat back in his chair.

"Ok," Jenny said. Tim has let us know what information he will need to be able to make some decisions. Who else has any ideas about what they might need to know in order to even consider moving forward?"

Each department head raised the issues he or she thought would be important to discuss, and Lori carefully wrote each one down. When they had run out of ideas, Jenny asked Lori to get a copy to each of them, and reminded everyone that together they would make the decisions about moving forward. When everyone left the meeting it seemed clear that hurt feelings had been soothed, and everyone was ready to move forward, but Jenny had no idea where forward was. She thought that Raj was probably ready to start working on a prototype, but for all she knew he already had one.

Where to start was going to be difficult for this group.

Chapter 8

The morning of their next meeting they were surprised to find another pencil on the table. They groaned aloud as this time Brian picked it up. "Design Products," was the message.

Brian tossed it to Raj. "This is yours, buddy," he laughed.

Jenny was pleased to see that at least one of her department heads had found their sense of humor.

"That's easy," Raj said. "My guys could do this in a week!"

"You mean you wouldn't want any of us to be involved?" Maya asked.

"No," Raj said. "This is just an R&D project. No one else is needed."

"Well," asked Olga, "how will you find out what the customers might like in a "SmartKiloPower" system?"

Raj replied, "They will either want it or they won't! What do you mean?"

"Well," Olga replied, "what is the maximum size this thing should be? Also, you should design it using as many common parts as you can with the "SmartMegaPower" system to simplify manufacturing."

"And purchasing," added Maya.

"And the production ought to use the same skills as the manufacturing of the "Mega," said Dave, abbreviating the name for ease of speaking. "That will simplify training."

"Can you do that, Raj?" Jenny asked.

"I don't know," Raj admitted. "I really hadn't thought about it.

"Well, you ought to think about it now," exclaimed Val. "And as you are thinking about it, keep in mind that it will have to be cheap!"

Raj looked like he was deep in thought. "Can all of you please think about these issues this week, and send me a list of all of your concerns so we can consider them during the design phase? I really just thought of design like this pencil, that I just had to design the product, but you are all making me think that design is much more than that."

Raj looked a bit worried.

Chapter 9

Jenny hadn't thought about Paul and his mural for a couple of weeks, but the following Monday, when she walked into the cafeteria at 9 in the morning, she got a big surprise when she saw a burst of color on the cafeteria wall. It was clearly just the background of the mural Paul was planning, and it was a dark gray rectangle in the middle of one large wall. It was about twenty feet wide and fifteen feet tall, and gave no hint of what he intended as the design.

She felt a little guilty that she hadn't thought about the mural at all, or even noticed that it wasn't coming into shape, but she acknowledged that she had been a little focused on other issues, and refused to feel guilty.

The agenda for this morning's meeting clearly needed to be the "SmartKiloPower" system.

Olga started the discussion. "We need to design the best product we can, test it with a few of our people, see how they use it and make sure it works before we even think about offering it for sale."

Jenny smiled as she was reminded of Steve Jobs at Apple. She had read that he said that they never wasted time asking customers what they wanted, they just worked on developing the coolest products they could make, and then everyone wanted them. Surveys couldn't really help when you were developing products that world had never seen before.

She turned to Raj. "Raj, tell us more about the SKP project.

"Well, as you know, the Mega system has enabled the strong growth of the company. The basic idea of the system is that it is a networked traffic controller for energy utilities to control the efficient generation and distribution of electricity. It consists of a network of software programs linked to the entire power generation and distribution system. It uses intelligent network agents to control the generation, routing and rerouting of power to meet the fluctuating needs of energy consumers on a real time basis. This product is produced in accordance with the specific requirements of each individual energy utility and every product is uniquely configured to order."

"Based on our success with the Mega system we identified the opportunity to use the same energy controller concept for SKP for individual residential and small businesses consumers. Our designers and programmers are waiting for your input into the product design before they develop it and test it at a couple of sites. Once they get the bugs out of the system we hope to introduce a test version to a sample market area within the next year."

It was no coincidence that Brian had tossed him the pencil that said "Design Products". Raj knew that these two simple words were critical to the success of this project and of the company and he was worried. He was feeling the awful weight of responsibility. He had studied hard at a prestigious engineering school and finished in the top five of his class, but this project wasn't just academic. It would be judged by the marketplace, and if it was successful the company would thrive and grow. If not, then his reputation would be shot, and depending on how much they invested, the whole company could be at risk of going out of business.

He knew all the right buzzwords. After receiving all of the input from the executive team he made sure that he covered everything they had suggested in addition to what he already understood. He included concurrent engineering, early supplier involvement, design teams, designing out fail points, poke yoke, house of quality, and every single one of the other things he had to design for. He was a qualified electrical engineer, and had read all the books, but this was his first actual independent project, and the prospect was both exciting and horrifying at the same time.

When he first joined the Lightning Bolt Company he spent time reading everything he could find on all the previous Lightning Bolt Company projects and he had documented all the reasons why any project had failed.

One project failure was because the product hardware enabled customers to choose whether or not to include a disk drive. If the customer chose not to have the disk drive then the disk drive bay was covered with a cover plate. Sales had forecast that the first year's sales would be 5,000. Purchasing had ordered 20,000 cover plates to get the lowest unit price possible. When the cover plates arrived they were too large for the disk drive bay. Since they had arrived one day before the product launch, there was no time to get the problem fixed. One very creative person suggested they could use super glue to hold them in place. This didn't do much for the appearance of the product since the screw holes were left empty, but this was how the product was demonstrated at the show. Needless to say the market was underwhelmed, and the company ended up scrapping the product, wasting a considerable sum of money. This was exactly the kind of design fiasco that Raj was determined would not be repeated.

He told the team about all the design criteria he knew: DFA meant Design for Assembly, DFQ meant Design for Quality, DFM meant Design for

Manufacturing, DFS meant Design for Serviceability, DFR meant Design for Recyclability, DFE meant Design for the Environment, etc. He made sure to stress that a lot of potential problems could be eliminated by doing an effective job in the design stage to make sure that products could be easily assembled, manufactured, serviced, and disassembled in the most effective way.

He opened his briefcase and displayed some products that had not been designed with the DF's in mind. He challenged the group to find the problem, and to suggest a solution.

One of the products, a bathroom scale, had a battery cover plate secured with one tiny screw. When you unscrewed it, it fell out on the floor, and without it the cover plate wouldn't stay closed.

When no one on the executive team even found the problem, he explained it and told them how pleased he was when one of his people came up with the idea of a sliding lock mechanism that avoided this problem.

He explained that he wanted to make sure that his people understood the concept of designing to a price point. He explained that in the 1970s an Asian manufacturer had purchased a commercial video tape recorder from an American company for $10,000. They recognized the opportunity. The Japanese manufacturer knew that if they could develop one for home use and sell it for $500, every family would want one.

The engineers took the machine apart, evaluated each of the component parts, and asked their people how they could manufacture a device like it for $400, so they could sell it for $500. They developed the world's first VCR and they had the whole market to themselves because their competition was still looking to the wrong market.

Raj explained that he wanted to set the same goal for his design group. While the Mega systems sold for tens of thousands of dollars, he told his designers they needed to develop the hardware and software for the SKP at a total package price of $400. He was sure that they could sell them for $500 to every home in the developed world.

He also wanted to make sure that they used the best concepts of modular design so they could sell to the global market, so he developed a House of Quality matrix which listed some possible customer requirements and linked them to technical requirements.

He was pleased that his designers had thought about producing a simple modular design for the SKP that would handle multiple input voltages and frequencies, with a standard output to power the device. He was also particularly proud of the concept of a flexible input adapter that could be changed to fit every type of electrical outlet in the world at the push of a button.

He had submitted this design for patent protection because it was so useful. Manufacturing would only have to produce one version regardless of the intended country of use which would make everyone's life easier. He had also directed the programmers to use modular code rather than custom code in the software which would make programming easier.

After Raj explained all of this to the executive team Jenny could see that they were as impressed as she was. They had all learned a lot through this process, even Raj, and if this project could be brought to fruition, he, with her team, would do it.

Chapter 10

Following their discussion on designing products everyone was feeling a little sorry for Raj. After all, he had the lion's share of the work in designing the SKP, and the rest of them could just keep on doing what they had always done.

Morning meetings focused on how the development of the SKP was coming along and on solving the normal problems that they had always had to deal with. It seemed clear that they were working much better as a team and Jenny found it less necessary to be glued to her office, her phone, and her to work in general.

The big gray rectangle, still on the cafeteria wall, was empty of further embellishments except for some shades of lighter colors around the edges to add texture to the background. Jenny knew that Paul was busy and she could see the results of his efforts elsewhere in the company. There was no question that the floor looked cleaner, the bathrooms were spotless, and the light fixtures actually seemed brighter.

One morning, shortly after their discussion on designing products, Brian arrived at work to find a colored pencil on his desk. He was staring at it when Jenny walked into his office.

"What is wrong?" she asked.

Brian pointed to his desk.

Jenny looked down, and after a moment of startled surprise, she picked it up. She smiled as she read the words that seemed so simple.

"Plan resources," she said. "Surely that is a BGO!"

"Sorry, BGO?" Brian replied. "I thought I knew most of the business acronyms, but I have never heard that one."

"It's OK," Jenny said. "It isn't really used by professional organizations, but it means a "Blinding Glimpse of the Obvious."

"Oh, I get it, it is a joke!" Brian, originally from Australia, was still trying to figure out what passed for humor in his new home country, and whenever he didn't understand something he would often ask people if they were joking.

"Yes, Brian," Jenny replied. "It is a joke, but then again, not really. Everyone knows that in business you need to plan resources, so that is what makes it obvious. The blinding glimpse part comes in when we realize that we haven't necessarily been doing a very good job of it."

She paused. "Do we do a very good job of it?" she asked, thoughtfully.

"Well," Brian replied. "The problem isn't as simple as it sounds. What do you mean by resources? I plan what I am going to buy and what I am going to make, but I think there are other resources that we use in the company that I have nothing to do with. For example, Dave plans the people resources, Val plans the money resources, and Tim plans the facility resources. Olga just sells stuff. We don't really plan our resources together.

Jenny thought for a moment, and then replied "Tell me what *you* plan and how you do it."

Brian walked over to his white board and took his black marker and drew a huge box and labeled it "ERP".

"You know that we have our Enterprise Resource Planning system that we just call "ERP," and that we use that system to manage all of our data. Basically it runs the whole company. It has information from our customers, our suppliers, on our products, on our people and our operations.

"Inside this box is another box called "Sales Forecast."

"My planning starts with the information that Olga gives me about what she has sold and what she thinks she is going to sell. She thinks that my job is just to make what she sells, and I understand that to the untrained person planning is the easiest job in the world. After all, all I have to do is balance supply with demand.

"My problem is that I don't really have any control over the demand, and as much as it might surprise you, I also don't have much control over the supply either! I order things that I need, but sometimes they don't arrive at all, much less on time, and sometimes when they do arrive they aren't exactly what I ordered or what I need. That doesn't matter, though, because ultimately I am accountable for the decisions that I make. When a planner makes a mistake it is obvious. It shows up in only one of two ways: excess inventory or product shortages, and sometimes they both occur at the same time. If a planner does a perfect job no one really notices, but if they make one mistake, everyone sees the impact!

"We start with the sales forecast that comes from Olga. That forecast includes the specific options required by the customers.

"We enter the forecast data, including the number of finished units predicted for customers into the planning system, along with any actual orders that came in from customers, which together become the Master

Production Schedule." Brian drew a second box, and labeled it "MPS."

"At the same time," and he drew a new box next to the second box, "we have rough cut capacity planning." He wrote the letters "RCCP" in the box.

"The purpose of Rough Cut Capacity Planning is to check the workload against the available capacity in critical work centers like Computer Numerical Control machines.

"If it is ok then we can continue the planning process." He drew another box, this one under the Master Production Schedule box. In this box he wrote "MRP".

"What does that mean?" Jenny asked.

"MRP stands for Material Requirements Planning and it is basically a huge calculator that takes every product Olga wants us to make and multiplies each product by every single component or raw material part that will be needed to produce the products that we are scheduled to make. We call that 'exploding the Bill of Materials.' That sounds like a lot of work, but no one does it manually anymore. We have computer programs that do this for us."

"So why do we have planners if the computers are doing all the work?" Jenny asked.

"We could let the computers do all the planning, and even let them automatically buy materials and issue work orders based on what is scheduled, and it might be a lot easier, but that only works when everything else is perfect. When things go wrong, and they often do for hundreds of reasons, you would have no one to ask why we have so much inventory of one thing, or why we ran out of another thing. You would have to ask the computer. Now, when you ask me why we have so many spools of red cable I can tell you that it is because Olga told us to make twenty additional units."

He was really pleased to have an opportunity to explain to her exactly what his people did on a daily basis.

"Every step is necessary. It is like a Russian nested doll. You start with a large one and after that is opened you find a smaller one beneath it and this continues until you finally reach the lowest level and smallest doll. This is exactly how planning works."

Jenny was staring at the diagram and suddenly she saw the problem with planning resources.

"You started with Olga's sales forecast, right?"

"Yes," Brian replied.

"Well, the sales plan was just a guess, and your planning system assumes it is absolutely right!"

"Yes, that is true," Brian agreed.

"Well, what happens if it is wrong?" Jenny asked.

"Then we have a planning nightmare, because all our plans were based on the ideal and unrealistic view that we live in a perfect world."

"You don't have to tell me what happens next," Jenny responded. "We spend far more money trying to get parts in on time to meet our promises, and we end up buying and building things that we don't really need, and we are always playing catch up when things change. I see the results in reduced profitability every single month end."

"Right," Brian said. "In my last job we looked stupid when one of our buyers expedited, de-expedited and re-expedited the same part on the same day all because our planning system was too nervous. The supplier just told us to sort it out and don't bother them until we got our act together."

Brian paused as he saw the realization on Jenny's face.

"The other problem is that my planners often resort to using their own personal spreadsheets to try and sort out what is really happening to fix what the computer says is happening. It is sometimes like juggling two bowling balls, a flaming torch and a sword while riding a unicycle."

"Planning is a nightmare!" Jenny explained. "I don't know why anyone in their right mind would want this kind of a job! I certainly don't, but I am glad that you are that crazy."

"I wasn't crazy before," Brian replied, "but this job has this effect on people."

Jenny stood up, turned to Brian and sincerely said "Thank you. I know we will talk about this some more, but I really appreciate your time," and left the room.

Chapter 11

At the next morning meeting Jenny asked Brian to tell everyone about the surprise he had received on his desk. Everyone was quite stunned, especially when they realized that the anonymous pencil pusher could actually target anyone with his or her "helpful hints."

"The conversation that Brian and I had after he received the pencil was really very helpful, and made me think that while Brian and his team do a great job of planning production and materials, he did make me aware that there are other resources that we either don't really plan, or that we plan separately. I wonder if we could either talk about resource planning in our morning meetings, or if perhaps there is a better way to do it. Have any of you had any experience of how it has been done helpfully somewhere else?"

Tim, usually one of the quiet ones at these meetings, spoke up.

"I don't usually have anything to share at these meetings, since I just take care of our building, but in my last job I was in sales. I hated sales, by the way, so Olga I can really appreciate the gift you bring to the job, but we had a monthly meeting where we just talked about resources. We called it the Sales and Operations Planning meeting."

"Who was there?" Jenny asked.

"Sales of course, since we knew what they had to make, and production since they were in charge of making it. Finance, since they knew about the financial resources that we had available, and planning since they had to procure most of the resources. Engineering because they were the experts in product definition, and HR was there because they knew the workforce availability. The CEO was always there since often high level decisions needed to be made and to resolve issues between sales and operations if they couldn't agree. In our company, that would mean Olga, Brian, Raj, Val, Dave and Jenny."

Jenny turned to the group. "What do you think?"

Olga, Val, and Brian were nodding, but Maya and Dave looked less sure.

"I am not really sure that I have anything to bring to the table," Dave said. "We only have 100 people here, and you know their schedules as well as I do. You might know them even better, since you know what they are planning before they make an official request of me, but I can come if you need me."

Maya said, "I am pretty much at the tail end of everything since I just ship what you make to the customer who ordered it, so I am not sure what I can bring to the process."

Jenny looked thoughtful. "Well, we already meet daily anyway, so I suppose we could allocate one of our mornings to trying it out and see how it works. How about getting together around the fifth or sixth of the month, after we have finished all the month end paperwork? We could just make that a continuation of our regular morning meeting, and if we needed Dave, Maya or Tim we could either ask them to stay, or call them to ask a question."

"Sounds right to me," Brian said, and Olga nodded. Tim, Maya, and Dave looked at each other and nodded as well.

Raj looked a little uncomfortable.

"Raj? What are you thinking?" Jenny asked.

"Well, I don't really want to be a problem, but I am really busy with the SKP project. I know how important that project is and will be to the company, so I wonder if I could either send someone else with the information on the product requirements, or if I could just keep you updated by email."

Jenny turned to Tim. "Tim? What do you think?"

"Well, here is an example," Tim replied. "Since the SKP project is so important, it will be the focus of almost everything we talk about in terms of resources. We will have to plan the personnel requirements, the capacity requirements, the financial projections, the sales campaign, and everything else. Until we had the conversation a couple of months ago, most of us didn't even know about the SKP project, so Raj has to be there to let us know what he is working on."

Turning to Dave, Jenny asked "Can you get Raj some help in managing this project?"

Dave turned to Raj. "Remember when we talked about needs? It seems like you have a need right now, for some help in your department. What would you need to feel a little less overwhelmed in managing this project?"

Raj looked thoughtful. "The project management is fairly straightforward, but I spend a lot of my time coding and checking code. I think I could really use another programmer, but can we afford it?"

Val replied "Yes, we can! Even with the expedited shipping and all the other extra expenses we had, that Barklay order put some extra money in our coffers, so I think we can afford that. Jenny?"

"Make it so, Dave. Raj, you give the job requirements to Dave, and let's see how fast we can make this happen. Does anyone have anything else?" Everyone shook their heads "no," so Jenny concluded, "OK, everyone. Have a great day!"

As everyone was getting up to leave, Lori turned to Jenny. "Can I have a minute?"

"Sure Lori, what's up?"

"I haven't every asked you about this because I didn't want to feel like I was using my relationship with you for anything personal, but my cousin Kent just lost his job with the Millennium nuclear power station when they closed, and this was exactly what he was doing. I wonder if he might be able to apply."

"Lori, I can't believe that you thought it wouldn't be right to ask for something as simple as this. Of course, he should apply! As a matter of fact, see if you can get him in today! I'll tell Dave. If he and Raj agree, Kent can be working tomorrow!"

"Oh, thank you!" smiled Lori. "That would be so amazing! I will call him right now."

Jenny grinned as Lori rushed out of the cafeteria. Being the CEO had its advantages, and if she could use her position to bring jobs to people, she was happy to do it.

Chapter 12

The next Monday Jenny's phone started ringing as soon as she dropped her handbag under her desk. She picked up the receiver. "Jenny Kim."

"Your so called smart products just shut down our entire power grid. We will be suing your company for breach of contract and we are going to hold you personally liable, and your company responsible for all the damages. People's lives are at risk. What the hell are you playing at?"

Jenny was totally taken aback. Nothing could have prepared her for this phone call. She struggled to take control of the conversation.

"Excuse me, but who is this please?"

"This is Bill St. Clair, from Atlantic Utilities, and until sixty seconds ago we relied on your so called SmartMegaPower system to get our power routed in the most efficient way possible, but right now there is NO POWER AT ALL! Prepare to hear from our lawyers!"

"I know that there must be a simple explanation," Jenny said. Give me your number and I will get my best engineer on the phone to help get you up and running immediately,"

"You do that right now. I will wait while you get them on the line."

Jenny called out to Lori, "Get Raj in my office right now!"

Lori was not used to Jenny barking out orders, but she knew it had to be critical, so she put her feelings aside, and called Raj. The call went straight to voice mail so she looked up his mobile number and sent him a text "URGENT Jenny's Office NOW!" His text came back within seconds, "Why?"

Lori texted back "System Outage Atlantic Utilities, holding on phone. Get here now!"

"OMG! ," was his response.

Less than one minutes later he came running in, and Jenny pointed to the phone as she switched the phone to speaker mode.

"Bill, I have Raj in my office. He is the head of my Engineering department. Bill, please, can you explain the situation?

Bill was practically screaming. "Your system caused a complete power outage in all our facilities. They were all shutdown at the same time. What the hell happened?"

"I am not sure," Raj said, "but I will pull up your data and run a remote diagnostic now. We should be able to get you back online very quickly once we isolate the problem. It could be a data issue, an operations issue or an equipment issue, and until I know, I can't say for sure how long it will take, but the faster I get the diagnostics running the better. Do you want to hold?"

"No," Bill said. "Just make it quick! We are dead in the water here."

"Ok," Raj said. "Expect my call in less than five minutes."

Jenny hung up the phone and turned to Raj. "What do you need to get this fixed?"

"Let me check into it. Can I use your computer?"

"Of course," Jenny replied and logged out, offering Raj her chair, desk, and office.

Raj logged into the network and pulled up the diagnostic site that allowed him access to all the customer sites. He searched by customer name and came up with the account, and ran the diagnostic program. Sure enough he noticed there was an unusual error code on the program, "Error 26 data value exceeds possible range."

"What the hell does that mean?" Raj asked out loud, not really expecting an answer from his boss. He wondered if programmers took some great delight in creating error codes and help messages that were obscure to the point of being useless.

He reached for his phone and sent an urgent text to his senior programmer, Jill, and within seconds he got the response. "My son is ill. Have to go to the doctors at 10:00."

"Call me now!" Raj texted.

A moment later his cell phone rang and he brought Jill up to speed. She logged into the diagnostic site on her home computer and they started a chat session.

"This means that there is a mismatch between their data and the expected range that was programmed into our system, probably because there is a version conflict between the two systems. Someone did an update to one without testing the impact on the other. Let me see if I can discover what happened."

Jill searched through the system history and discovered the exact moment when the problem had occurred. Someone at Atlantic Utilities had run an update program to their system without running a compatibility check, even though the installation instructions clearly said that the compatibility check was a <u>requirement</u> before any update. It was a fairly simple fix. She just had to initiate a system rollback to the conditions that existed before the update was applied and then the error code disappeared.

"Should be OK now," she said.

"You are a miracle worker," Raj replied, and he hung up his phone.

Jenny called Bill, who answered immediately. She told him that they had fixed the problem, and Bill replied that he was already seeing the power stations coming back on line.

"Thank you for taking such quick action," Bill said, "but I want a complete report of what went wrong and what corrective actions are necessary to ensure this never happens again!"

Jenny said "So do I. We will make this our top priority and we will have a full report to you within 48 hours."

Bill thanked her and hung up the phone, and Jenny and Raj looked at each other.

"Hell of a way to start the morning!" Jenny said. "Why don't we grab a coffee and see if we can sort this out!"

They went to the cafeteria and as they sat down at their usual table they saw the pencil sitting on the desk. Neither of them reached for it, but Jenny could read it right on the table. It said "Assure Quality."

"You know," Jenny said, "I am getting more than a little bit fed up that someone knows more than we do about what is going on around here. I don't know who is leaving these pencils around, but I sure wish they would just show their face and tell us what the heck we need to do!"

Raj replied, "You know we don't have anyone in charge of Quality. Maybe that is the problem."

"No," Jenny replied. "I have worked with Quality departments. They are just a bunch of people who made somewhat arbitrary decisions about what products were good and what were bad. They didn't really help create quality products, they simply acted as judges deciding what products not to send to customers. Most problems they identified were design issues, process issues, material issues or training issues, and they didn't actually fix any of them."

Raj said "Well, somehow we need to come up with a more thorough way of testing our programs before we send them out into the field. I have been thinking about our testing process and today we saw a real-life situation that confirms that the process isn't working. Before we issue any updated version of our software we run through all the tests we can on our system, but we have no way of checking to see what on site modifications the customer may have made. The system works in all kinds of different environments, but each customer can make their own modifications once they buy it. Then when we release software updates they can cause the kind of problem we experienced this morning if the customer doesn't do the compatibility check before they activate the update."

Jenny replied, "I don't mind investing in preventing problems, but I don't want a department of product judges. These people add no value in the mind of the customer. I think we should have testing processes that ensures that it is impossible to release products that can create the kind of damage we experienced today."

Raj said "I will take that as an immediate priority and get back to you when I have a solution and I will write the corrective action report for Bill."

"Great. Let's use the problem as an opportunity to talk with the team about quality later."

Jenny walked back to her office conflicted about whether the morning had been a bad dream or a wake-up call.

Chapter 13

At the team meeting Jenny saw the group passing around yet another pencil.

"Ok," she asked. "What does this one say?"

"Improve Processes," said Maya.

Jenny chuckled. "Right on time," she said, and she briefly explained the crisis, the resolution, and the dilemma she and Raj had faced with regard to how to manage software updates.

"I think we can improve the quality of our initial software as well as the quality of our updates, but it looks like the process by which we update the software seems to be ineffective. Somehow quality and processes seem to be linked, and no one here is in charge of that."

"Well," Tim said, "really we all are responsible for it. It all starts with recognizing what a process is, seeing our work as a series of processes that link our work with the work of others. Every single person in the company is responsible for their own work processes, how they link to the processes of others, and for making sure that the work they pass on to someone else is the highest possible quality. Olga and Maya are responsible for the processes that link our work with the work of our customers, and so they are responsible for the quality of those processes. Brian and Raj are responsible for the processes that link our work to that of our suppliers and customers and so they are responsible for that quality.

"Everything we do takes inputs from somewhere, does something to them, and then takes the output and passes it on to someone else, our customer. If we haven't talked to that someone else about our work, we might never know if there is something we are doing that could be improved, or could be stopped entirely. We don't need a quality department to take charge of that. We need to take charge of it ourselves."

Jenny asked, "I know that we meet regularly, and we talk often about what is happening with our own departments, but do our people talk with each other?"

"Sometimes," said Maya. "Olga and I have lunch regularly, and Lori and Kent do now that he is here."

Brian waved around the cafeteria and said "I see and hear lots of conversation here in the cafeteria during breaks and lunch so I suspect our people talk to each other about a lot of things having to do with work."

"I wonder," Jenny asked, "if any of them have any ideas about how we could do things smarter?"

"Probably," Val laughed. "All we would have to do is to give them the opportunity to tell us."

"Perhaps we should do that," Jenny commented. "Let's set up a suggestion box asking for ideas about how we can improve our internal processes, and see what happens."

"Get ready to hear a lot of crazy ideas!" added Val.

Jenny said "For the next few days let's take a look at everything we are doing and see if there are ways we can do it better or smarter. Olga, you should check with your order entry people. They might have some good ideas like the one we had about asking about inspections and other activities that might interfere with installation. Brian, I will give someone $1000 if they can come up with a great money-saving idea in production, and the same in any of your departments. If we can do things smarter and save money in the process, we will be that much further ahead.

"Raj, I know you are going to work on the software to include a compatibility test that will run before the upgrade. Perhaps Kent has some other ideas that we can include in our software, and Maya, talk with some of our customers and see if there is something we can do to make delivery go more smoothly. Tim, I am not sure what you can do to make things work more efficiently in the building, but keep your eyes open, and Val, see what kind of a budget we can come up with to support all this!"

Despite each of her department heads already being fully employed, she actually saw some enthusiasm in their faces for the idea of looking at everything as a process and then improving the processes.

Things at the Lightning Bolt Company just kept getting better and better.

Chapter 14

Olga walked into her office and found herself the lucky winner of the colored pencil game. She picked up her gift and quickly read the two words "Manage Demand."

"Easier said than done," was her initial reaction. "We don't manage demand at all, we *guess* demand." She was painfully aware that she had virtually no ability to predict demand accurately or control the way customers placed orders. The Barklay order had proven that. She had been working on getting their business for nearly two years, and then all of a sudden she got an order for twenty units.

She had often fantasized about working in a company that was so responsive that they could actually ship products before the customers changed their minds. Her world would be so much easier working for a pizza company with a 30-minute lead time from order receipt to delivery. Her world wasn't like that. It took approximately two weeks to build each Mega system, and all kinds of order changes could occur in that time frame. Planning problems started with the assumption that the sales forecast was correct, and while she tried to be as accurate as possible, this hardly ever happened.

She knew that Brian had often been bitten by lousy forecasts, and knew that he did what every planning manager did, "buy double to stay out of trouble." They both knew that this only made things worse since you could get into trouble for having too much inventory, but that was better than getting into trouble for not being able to ship products on time.

In recent years it seemed that the problem was getting worse. Customers were more demanding than ever before. Brian told her that suppliers were reluctant to hold inventory and that supply lines were getting longer owing to offshore sourcing. There was simply more risk inherent in the system. The whole world was searching for the highest value at the lowest price, and this didn't help quality or customer service. Brian was convinced that the level and quality of service was going downhill rapidly as companies focused on profit and looked to save money by reducing costs for material and labor.

Olga was well aware of the three elements of demand management. The first was called CRM, or Customer Relationship Management. She wasn't a big fan of CRM. She thought it pushed you to discriminating between customers on the basis of how important they were, as if one person had more value than another. She had seen situations where different customers got different treatment, and it didn't sit well with her. Who should decide which customer should get a cancer-treating drug? It seemed very unfair that rich customers could afford the treatments, but poor customer could not. She had also experienced first-hand where the biggest customer was also the worst customer.

She had worked for a company where more than sixty percent of their gross sales revenue came from one customer. When this customer wanted anything, they got it, often at the expense of other customers. The customer knew this and often placed unreasonable demands on her company. She believed every customer was important and she objected to the notion that some customers were more important than others.

The second area of demand management was Sales Forecasting, and this was definitely not an exact science. Sure, there were university professors who explain the underlying statistical nature of forecasts with all kinds of mathematical formulas, graphs, and algorithms, but in the end it didn't matter which method was used. The only question that remained was how it would be wrong.

Individual customers never followed normal distribution patterns. Demand was inherently unpredictable, and while she recognized that some products had more demand stability than others, some products were very difficult to forecast. She knew that for many products historical sales data was relevant. She thought about the SKP and realized that this brand new product had no historical data, and wouldn't during its introduction phase, so that simply wasn't available.

In many cases the previous sales history of a product was irrelevant. If a product becomes an instant hit on social media, sales could go through the roof instantly, and stop just as quickly.

At school the professors told her that the best forecasts would predict a likely range of demand from a low side to a high side, but planning systems don't allow you to plan for a range of demand. Systems want a number, so planners would compensate by building "just in case inventory" of safety stock to manage any high demand variation. In reality safety stock was a misnomer since there was no level of safety stock that could guarantee perfect customer service. Any customer could place an order that would create a backorder. All they had to do was order a few more products than you had available.

The third area was Order Fulfillment, and this dealt with how you handled real orders for products or services from customers. When a customer is searching for a product to buy, they can visit stores, they can shop online or they can ask their friends for recommendations. This is all "pre-sales" activity, but when the customer decides what to buy, then they enter into a sales contract with a supplier. If the product is on the shelf in a store, they simply remove it from the shelf, take it to a cashier and the sales transaction consists of a simple exchange of cash or a credit card charge. The order fulfillment process is complete.

If they shop online they can buy products at any time of the day or night. They immediately receive an automated response from the supplier that acknowledges the receipt of the order, but nothing actually happens until the next business day. The customer has no idea where in the world the supplier is located, or what time zone the supplier is in, and only gets valuable information when they receive a shipping notification. The shipping notification indicates that a product has been shipped, and might include a tracking number that can be used to identify where the product is and when delivery will occur.

In the mind of the customer the lead time clock is ticking from the moment the order is placed until the product is actually received, and if there is a problem, the lead time clock is still ticking until the problem is resolved.

Olga knew all about demand management, but it still didn't help her. Maya was always hounding Brian for products that were late.

They all knew that customer service numbers could be improved, but she had no idea how to do it. Some months she got lucky and the numbers looked better than others, but she had no way of creating a process improvement project on her own. It seemed like customer service was simply a game of chance, and she wished she had a way to systematically and consistently strive towards a target of improved customer service. So far she hadn't found it. Perhaps the team could help.

Chapter 15

At their next meeting the group was surprised to find that there had been some additions to the mural on the wall! The background now had a lot of texture that was provided by shading, and they could see the outline of a circle in the middle that was about six feet across. A series of black lines branched out from the circle.

"It looks like a flower," Maya speculated.

"I think it is a bicycle wheel," offered Tim.

"How about the bottom of a blender?" chuckled Raj.

"Or a windmill," said Olga.

"A fan," said Brian.

"Speaking of fans," Val said, "one of the suggestions we got was to provide fans in the production department. It seems that some of our workers don't appreciate the level of heat generated by our production process, and they would like fans to cool the area off."

"I usually go there early in the morning, just to have a look around, and it isn't hot then. Brian, does the factory get hot?" Jenny asked.

Brian blushed, beneath his brown skin. "I am from Perth in Australia, and I am used to being hot. I never thought about it, but I guess that it might be too hot for some. Could we put in exhaust fans in the roof?" This was directed at Tim.

"Sure," Tim replied. I would have to get a climate engineer to tell me how many fans of what size I would need to help lower the temperature, but I am sure it could be done."

"Can we get that information without committing to a particular contract?" Val asked.

"Probably," Tim replied. Do you want me to check in to it?

"Jenny?" Val looked at Jenny.

"Please," Jenny replied. "Did anyone else get any good suggestions?

"Actually yes," replied Raj. "We have been doing our programming when we receive an order from a customer. Right now we know that there are a limited number of different software configurations customers need, so Kent suggested that we merge the software and configure it through the use of switches. It would save us tons of programming hours once we got it done, so I have asked him to head that up. Lori, your cousin is practically a clone of me, and I am so very glad that you told us about him."

Lori blushed. "He loves working here, and feels like he has found a great home, so thank you for giving him a chance."

"What is next to talk about," Jenny asked.

"I got a pencil," Olga said.

Everyone turned to her.

"What? You waited this long to tell us?" Maya exclaimed.

"Well, we were all talking about suggestions, and I didn't want to interrupt." She pulled the pencil out of the bundle of hair in her clip. "Manage Demand," she said.

Silence once again prevailed.

"SKP," Brian said. "We don't have any idea what the demand will be for SKP, so how can we possibly manage it. We do fine with Mega, except for those crazy last minute orders," he cast a sharp look at Olga, "but we have no idea what we demand we will have for SKP."

Jenny looked around, and said "You are right, this is going to be a challenge, but we will just have to cross that bridge when we come to it. What have we learned so far?

"We know how important it is for us to work together as a team and share our knowledge and skills to achieve results. We know that we have to be vigilant in terms of identifying not only the needs of our customers, but also our own needs, both personal and professional. We know that our product design has to include not only what we think the customer wants, but also what we can source, produce and maintain easily and efficiently. We know that we are ultimately responsible for the quality of our products but also for the processes we use to produce them and to facilitate transactions with our customers and our suppliers. We know that we have to be thoughtful about planning all of the resources we rely on to conduct our work, whether internal or external, people, materials, machines, and our work environment. We also know that we will have to be careful not to overwhelm ourselves as we try to produce, test, market, make and then manage the demand for SKP. We just have to keep our heads about us, continue to prepare for all eventualities and still take care of the demands of each day. I value each one of you, and I know we can do it."

Jenny didn't ordinarily go in for pep talks, but these were her sincere thoughts, and she knew that the team

had been through a lot. She also wanted them to know
that she truly did value them.

Chapter 16

Val was concerned about the future of the SKP project. She knew that Raj and his engineers were working hard on the new product, but she was worried about how much information she would need to input into the Enterprise Resource Planning (ERP) system in order for it to support the delivery of SKP.

On her way to work she had been thinking about the Item Master file which had over 100 data entry fields. Decisions would have to be made about what type of information would be loaded into each field. She knew that the engineering department typically worked on new product development independently. The engineers would work on a project, and when they had finished they would "throw it over the wall" to the rest of the company, and then the rest of the company had to try to figure out how to bring the product to market, make it, deliver it, and account for the income and expense. It all happened in a vacuum.

Engineers sometimes had a certain level of arrogance, the kind that sometimes comes from people in an exclusive profession. They tended to dismiss ideas from people outside their field of expertise, and it didn't help that she was a woman and they were all men.

When she took this job she believed that it would be different, but she didn't see any evidence that Raj was seeking input from the rest of the company.

She wondered how to approach Raj to try to get him to open up the project so she could get the data she needed to do the required work to get the ERP system ready for SKP.

"Is this a need?" she wondered.

She thought that Raj might consider her requirements an intrusion. She knew he was under a lot of pressure to deliver the project, and thought that he would probably be disturbed by anything that he perceived added to his work load, slowed him down or put the project at risk.

It was definitely not a simple problem, she reflected.

Traditionally engineers thought of their skills as "hard skills," those related to science and technology. They looked at her and her skills as soft skills, those related to dollars and people. Val thought that these definitions were completely reversed. In her experience dealing with people was infinitely harder than dealing with machines. Machines, in particular computers, did as they were told. They performed the way they had been programmed. People did not.

Val saw the world through the eyes of an accountant. Numbers were her friends! She tended to think in spreadsheets.

There were three levels of value in her world of numbers. The lowest level was data; just facts that were collected by the computer system every minute of every day. Every order that was placed, every movement of product from one work station to another, every invoice and dollar of income was recorded and safely stored in their computer system. Separately these points of information were just that, single points of data.

From it she could extract valuable information using search routines, and exception reports. She could ask "what if" questions and run simulations. She could prepare management reports based on various scenarios, or she could run reports based on actual historical data. She felt important and necessary. In her professional life Val had always had access to Google, and she was as comfortable extracting information from the Internet as she was from her system at work. Data became information in the right hands, but she knew there was an even higher level of information that was extremely valuable to the company. That level was the level of intelligence.

At this level, it was essential to find that single piece of vital information that when it got to the right person at the right time could win the war. Intelligence had the power to change history.

One of her favorite movies was "Back to the Future," and she often wished she could travel in time. It would be so cool to go back in time and invest in the stock market when you had valuable intelligence about the future. She would definitely have purchased all the Google and Amazon stock that she could afford.

Somehow she was not surprised when she arrived in her office to find a pencil on her desk. The words "Validate Information" were written on it.

She put down her coat, picked up the pencil, and walked to Olga's office. With her knock on the open door, Olga lifted her eyes from the report on her desk.

"You busy?" Val asked.

"You don't really expect me to answer that, do you?" Olga replied. "I'm not happy with any of the possible sales forecasts for SKP. I am concerned that I have no idea how many units we are going to sell. We have no sales history. It is a completely different product from the Mega, with a completely different market, completely different customers, and sold in a completely different way. I don't want to be overly optimistic or unduly pessimistic."

"Right," Val said, "and any mistake in the forecast will cost us money that we can't afford. That is partly the reason I am here. I really need everyone to be as realistic as possible. I got a pencil today," Val said. "It said 'Validate Information'."

"So," Olga replied. "We are both working on the same kind of thing and the pencil tells us that it is the right thing to be working on. Do you have any ideas about how I can get the right information?"

Val thought for a moment. "It isn't an easy problem. You are going to have to do develop a model for all the possible factors that will drive SKP sales. I have a very similar problem. I have to prepare budgets on income and expense projections, and I don't have either!

"I was thinking that the best approach would be to start with a very conservative forecast as the SKP is introduced, and to limit the introduction to a test market to see what kind of reactions we get from the first customers. That makes my job a bit more difficult since in my experience the introductory costs per unit are much higher than in the mature phase of the market, so to price the SKP to facilitate future sales we might have to lose money during introduction. It won't be easy at first, but it should get more accurate as we get more experience from the market."

Olga said "That's a good idea. I think I will present a range of three forecast numbers for each month: a pessimistic one at the low end of the range, one that is most likely and one that is optimistic at the high end of the range. Then you can develop the income and expense projections for each, and Brian can choose which numbers he wants to go with for production."

"That sounds like a great plan," Val replied. "Now, perhaps you give me some advice on how to handle my problem with how to validate information if you are not too busy!"

"Sure," Olga said. "What do you need?"

"Well, I need to make sure that we have all the relevant SKP data loaded into our master files before we can start planning, buying, making, costing, and selling the SKP. There is an awful lot of information that is either missing, hasn't been decided or is subject to change. It is always like this with a new product. The dilemma is always about speed versus completeness. If I wait until all the data is fully defined then the information won't be available for use until I get it loaded. If I enter only the information that I have now, then the information won't be complete and any scenario data will be suspect. The challenge is how to get the right information entered into the system as quickly as possible."

"Well, where does that information come from?" Olga asked.

"Initially the design information comes from Raj's group, but they don't know the details of any other business function. Brian needs to source all the components for the new product from the design and give me the details on suppliers, lot sizes and lead times for all the components. Then I can start developing the product cost. We really need to get everyone together to try and figure out all the pieces like lot sizes, most product configurations, material requirements, and so forth."

"Sounds like a good topic for this morning's meeting," Olga replied. "By the way, we are five minutes late already!"

Chapter 17

The group entered the cafeteria to find that there was more definition in the mural. A new and smaller circle had been added in the middle of the original circle, and what looked like little triangles projected into it from what they had decided to call "spokes."

"Looking more like a flower," Maya said. "Look at the petals forming in the middle of the outside circle!"

"Nah," replied Tim. "It looks even more like a bicycle wheel. Those triangles are the gears on the chain."

Val interjected "I got a pencil!" That, of course, got everyone's attention.

Jenny held out her hand. "Lay it on us," she said.

Val handed Jenny the pencil. "Validate Information," Jenny read out loud.

"I don't want to throw a monkey wrench into the works," Val said, "but Olga and I have been talking, and it seems that this is an issue for both of us right now. I think we have resolved Olga's problem, but let's share what we came up with. Olga?"

Olga took over, and told the group what she and Val had decided was a reasonable forecast approach to pass to Brian and that they had agreed that he had to make the call based on his assessment of how many units he thought he could produce.

Val continued. "My job is to develop financial data for you to look at based on cost estimates for each sales forecast, and thereby derive potential profit or loss figures. Once we have those, we can decide whether or not to move forward."

"That makes great sense," Jenny offered.

"There is only one snag," Val said, sneaking a look at Raj. "For cost data, I will need the SKP bill of materials."

As expected, Raj blew up. "Like I don't already have enough pressure on me! We are working as hard and as fast as we can to develop the product, and we haven't even determined the final design specifications, and you want the bill of materials now!"

"Not exactly," countered Val, trying to keep her voice calm and her demeanor collected. "I do know that you are under an extraordinary amount of pressure, and may not have all the data yet, but if there is any data that you do have, I could get it loaded into the system know, and Brian can start sourcing it."

Raj must have been practicing meditation under pressure, because he came down from his energized explosion fairly quickly.

"There is some information that we have," he acknowledged. I can get that to you now, and I can feed you information as we get it, as long as you don't blow up at me if I have to change something later."

Val breathed a sigh of relief. "Actually, that sounds wonderful," she replied.

"Once again, our team succeeds in navigating the turbulent waters!" Jenny affirmed. "Well done. Ok everyone, is there anything else?"

"Yes," Brian replied. "Tim and I have spoken with several contractors and picked the one we want to implement the rooftop exhaust fans. Interestingly, when the workers saw the contractors crawling over the roof they realized that we were serious about making the change, and they have been quite enthusiastic. I think that there has actually been an improvement in productivity as a result."

"That is great news. Thank you both," Jenny replied. "Ok, team. Have a great day!"

As the team left the cafeteria, Jenny looked at the mural, speculatively. "I wonder?" she said to herself, and she looked at the pencil.

Chapter 18

The next pencil was a gift to Brian, and before he shared it with the team he spent a good deal of time thinking about it.

It simply said "Maximize flow."

He was in the shower and was thinking about work and how work should flow just like the water in the shower. He remembered his first visit to Niagara Falls. He had heard about it when he was a child growing up in Australia, where it rains very little.

When he took his first vacation after moving to America, he drove to into Canada to see Niagara Falls from the Canadian side. As he walked through the town he found that he could hear the falls long before he could actually see them. When he walked up to the edge of the overlook and saw the enormous amount of water that flowed over the falls he simply couldn't comprehend where it was all coming from. He had seen a map and knew that the Great Lakes existed. He knew that they were emptying into Lake Ontario by way of the Niagara River, but he couldn't conceive of a source of the water that was so very unending. A local guide showed him a map of the watersheds in North America and explained that all the water was coming from the Rocky Mountains. The guide pointed out the continental divide and showed him the rivers flowing into and through the Great Lakes and then down the St. Lawrence River, to drain into the Atlantic Ocean.

Water was the ultimate renewable resource. Like energy, it could be neither created nor destroyed. It simply changed from one form to another. It could evaporate into a gas, it could condense into a liquid, and it could become solid as ice. Water was the perfect commodity. It was always in demand, was essential to life, and was constantly renewed. The key was to find the right source and then find a way to market it and distribute it. He had been amazed at the market for bottled water even when everyone had clean water piped right into their homes.

Now he thought about the production flow as though he were a plumber. He wondered if he could create a product pipeline with valves and meters to control the flow of SKP to market. He would start with the end user of the product. If a meter were installed that would monitor the rate at which SKPs were consumed, this would set the rate at which the supply should be replenished. Then he would set up a supply pipeline that would be tightly controlled using a valve that could be opened or closed depending upon the exact rate at which customers needed the product. He had heard of something like this before. It was called

Demand Driven Planning. From what he knew, it was very effective at ensuring the right products were delivered to the right customers at the right time.

He could see how it might resolve his problems with planning everything based on a sales forecast that everyone knew was prone to error. That error, in the case of the Mega system, was compounded by the Mega's having a 42 day lead time, and during this lead time the forecast might change considerably.

He had identified the longest lead time components and had arranged to carry safety stock on these items, but this didn't always work because sometimes the forecast was so different from actual sales that he had no way to dynamically adjust the amount of safety stock.

He knew that all Enterprise Resource Planning (ERP) systems started with the same planning logic, which was based on a set of assumptions that may have been valid five decades ago, but certainly didn't work in the business world today. He smiled to himself as he thought about all the things that the planning system assumed: that the forecast was right, that customers always place orders with sufficient lead time, that customers never change their minds, that all the data in the system was correct, that the inventory numbers in the system were exact, that every supplier delivered on time and no incoming deliveries were ever rejected, that production always gets it right and that nothing ever went wrong. He would have liked to reduce the lead time, but he didn't know how to do this. Planning, really only worked in fantasy, it certainly didn't work in his world.

He had attended a Demand Driven Planning course and had been impressed by the concept of placing cushions at key points. They would absorb normal variation in the same way that shock absorbers work in a car to provide a smooth ride over all the potholes and obstacles that can occur when driving down a street. The Lightning Bolt Company was dealing with huge potholes and barriers to smooth product flow, so he welcomed anything that could promote smoother product flow to customers. He truly wanted to ensure that every product got shipped to the right customer on time every time.

He had recently established their "perfect order metric" according to the SCOR (Supply Chain Operations Reference) model. Their current level of perfect orders was about 1 in 3.

He knew that some companies had achieved an amazing level of shipping reliability; in some cases they could measure their performance to a level of six sigma which was less than four imperfect orders in a million. Somehow that seemed a long way off for him.

The next day he called the instructor for the Demand Driven Planning course he had taken, and was referred to a software company. The marketing manager agreed to provide a free simulation tool that he could use to see if there was something that he could do to reduce their lead time.

Within the next ten days, Brian had shared his plumbing and Niagara Falls story with the executive team, along with the "Maximize Flow" message and he had run several product simulations using the tool from the software supplier. He had proven to himself that it was possible to compress the lead times on the Mega system from 42 days down to 16 days, which would make the whole demand system less volatile. He had decided where he needed to place strategic inventory buffers to absorb fluctuating demand and supply side variability. He estimated that he could even reduce the inventory of raw materials and component parts by 30% from the current level, saving money, and he could adjust the inventory buffers as required.

The best thing about all of this is that he would no longer be held at the mercy of the inaccurate sales forecast. He definitely liked the word "flow," and he knew that if the company maximized the rate of product flow to the customer, then inevitably this would create the maximum rate of cash flow into the company.

With that logic, he talked the team into doing it and within two weeks the software was installed, his team trained, and the savings were already showing up in reduced inventory.

Chapter 19

Jenny noticed the next pencil as she entered her office. She was meticulously organized. At the end of each day she had the habit of clearing everything off her desk so that she could make a fresh start the next business day. She couldn't work in a cluttered workspace. Her whole house, apart from Su's room, was organized and she took great pleasure in knowing that there was a place for everything and everything was in its place. It was very attractive and had also been arranged for the minimum amount of effort and few wasted motions.

She used that the same practice at work, and she had decided to challenge the Executive Team to take photos of each workspace and have a prize for the department that had cleaned and tidied their area the best. To Jenny, part of improving processes was the creation of the ideal workspace.

She would gladly be the judge, and she had already decided that the winning department would have a pizza party and everyone in the winning department would be entered into a contest to win an SKP unit.

Obviously the colored pencil on her otherwise clean desk was something that offended Jenny's sense of order. The pencil should not just be lying there. It should be stored in accordance with how often it would be required for use, so she picked up the pencil and read "Build Networks."

"What on earth does that mean," she thought to herself. The Mega system enabled power utilities to run their own networks in the most effective way. Did the message mean that they should use their own technology to build their own internal power network?

Most people have a clearly defined notion of what is meant by "network." The easiest to relate to was the cable service provider who provides multiple channels of programming in addition to Internet services and phone services. A network could be a network of services, but it could also be a network of suppliers, a network of systems, a network of people, or a network of customers. Jenny didn't know what the pencil distributor had in mind for her, but she knew that everyone who had received a pencil had been challenged to think beyond their experience, so perhaps that was what she was being challenged to do.

She decided fairly quickly that it didn't mean putting in place computer networks, because they were already in place, and they had become such an indispensable part of day to day business life it was unlikely that their hidden business guide had that in mind.

She thought about the kind of networks that companies should have: internal and external.

Her parents had sent her to a prestigious university in London, and while she was there she experimented with setting up a transportation business. She had discovered an unmet need. Her fellow students wanted to be able to go home to their families during the breaks between semesters, but it was hugely expensive for them plus required multiple transfers between modes of transportation. Jenny thought through a design for a customized travel service for students. After getting in touch with friends in other universities she contracted with a private bus service and arranged transportation for groups of students between London and their homes when there were universities in or near their communities. Then she arranged transport for students from those universities to London. At the end of the semester break she would reverse the routes and get everyone back to school.

She advertised this customized travel service, sold tickets, and contracted for buses. This service, besides being nearly door to door, was much cheaper than existing transport. In essence, it was like the first Uber service.

Jenny filled the buses both ways and after expenses made enough profit to fund her travel around England on her own semester break. It seemed like a win-win situation. The students were happy, their families were happy, the service was good, and it worked well. Unfortunately, the English Road Traffic Commissioner decided that she was competing with a nationalized industry, the publicly owned transport industry, and wrote to her demanding that she "cease and desist" all operations, so she stopped.

Jenny knew that her UK network consisted of transactions with multiple partners based on a contractual arrangement for the benefit of all.

She thought about a single transaction between a customer and a supplier. When she wanted toothpaste, for example, she could walk into any grocery store or drug store, pick it up off the shelf, pay for it, and walk out. There was no contract, no relationship, no long term obligation; it was just a simple purchase in a store, with no lasting effect on either the customer or the supplier.

She didn't want her business to be based on simple transactions, but rather lasting partnerships between her people and their customers and between her people and their suppliers. She really wanted lasting relationships with mutual benefit.

She had heard about the kind of supplier network that was employed by a car manufacturer. Essentially the manufacturer treated their network of suppliers as an extension of their family. They used only one source for any given part for any given vehicle, and while there was some risk in that, the network of relationships meant that other suppliers would pitch in to help if there was a problem at any one supplier.

This was proven when a fire occurred at a one supplier's building that put that supplier out of commission for six months. The manufacturer sent out a message asking for help from the other suppliers in the family. They sent out the design specifications for the part they needed and asked if any of their other suppliers had the capability to produce these parts.

Once they had evaluated the capability of the most likely replacement suppliers they asked for sample parts to be delivered. They selected the replacement supplier, redirected the raw materials to the new supplier, and were up and running in three days.

Thanks to their relationships with their supplier network they experienced minimal disruption, and when the company that had experienced the fire was back up and running, they got the business back. This was the kind of network of suppliers that Jenny wanted to have in place for the Lightning Bolt Company.

It was clear to her that she and her team needed to work on building these kinds of networks in order to ensure their future.

Chapter 20

Finally, at one morning meeting, Raj informed the team that he and his group had completed the design of the SKP unit and documented the required bill of materials and preliminary product routing information. The SKP had passed all the internal tests, and was ready to be sent out to some families for further testing.

Jenny declared a holiday for engineering. She told Raj to record a voice mail message telling all incoming callers that their office was closed for an inspection, and to send everyone home with pay. Brian was charged with developing the master schedule from the designs and getting the specifics to Val for entry into the ERP system, and then building units for external testing. Olga and Dave were charged with identifying some families to test the unit, and together with Maya they were to prepare to ship them out.

Everyone was totally focused on the SKP units, so it was a major shock when Olga returned to her office to find a message from Atlantic Utilities with an order for 80 Mega units as quickly as possible. She quickly called Jenny, and after reporting the order to her, they called Brian, Val, and Maya in.

"I know we are all excited about Raj's success with the SKP, but the Mega has been our bread and butter for years, and Olga just received an order for 80 units from Atlantic Utilities. You may remember that they are the company that had that incredible power outage recently because they committed to an update without running a compatibility check. Our rapid response in fixing the problem apparently won us a lot of good will, and a big order.

"I want to make it happen, so let's figure out what the next step is."

Brian responded by outlining his requirements. "Once again we will need to expedite the parts, and since it is for 80 units this time, we will need a bigger plane. I will need authorization for four times the overtime we used for the Barklay order. Fortunately this isn't a big vacation period, so I should have everyone at work."

Maya also had a requirement. "We simply don't have anywhere near the capacity in shipping to package and ship that many units. I will have to add another shipping shift and place a rush order for the packaging materials and see what contract terms I can get with the freight company for such a large order."

Val had some concerns. "The budget is right on track for the SKP, but we have committed our funds to that project without knowing that this order would require the outlay of a lot of cash expediting parts and paying overtime. It will be a while before we see any income from this sale. Without running the numbers I can say that I am quite sure that we are going to have to activate our line of credit at the bank."

Olga, enthusiastic for this extraordinary sale, turned to Jenny. "We have to do it!" she exclaimed. This is a huge opportunity for us to shine. No one has ever ordered 80 units from us before. Until now, the Barklay order of 20 units was the largest we had ever gotten!"

"Ok, everyone, do what has to be done, but let's make this happen!" Jenny replied.

The group dispersed, each to their own office, but Maya found her stomach in knots as she considered what this would mean for the entire company if it went bad.

The next two weeks were a nightmare. Jenny even cancelled the morning meeting to allow everyone the extra time to manage the huge amount of extra work.

Fortunately, Raj wasn't required for the Atlantic order, so he took over developing the manufacturing specifications for the SKP from Brian so Brian could concentrate on the Mega units.

Once Val had finalized the line of credit she was able to start paying the bills that were coming in, and at the same time she rushed the processing of entering the Enterprise Resource Planning (ERP) data that Raj was giving her.

Maya got fairly good contract terms from the freight company, and was fortunate enough to be able to get the shipping containers quickly, so she felt a little less pressure, but she still had the feeling that somewhere along the line something was going to go very wrong.

Finally, the first twenty units were ready for shipment, and the next twenty were just a couple of days behind with the last forty scheduled twenty at a time three days apart. Tempers were barely restrained, but no one came to blows, and Jenny felt like it was a big success until she found a pencil on her desk. "Communicate Intelligence" was the message.

She hadn't even had a chance to think about it when quiet, humble, down to earth Maya came storming into her office.

"Val just yelled at me!" she exclaimed. "She told me I was spending way too much on shipping and I had to stop, NOW! I can't do my job like this. You have to do something! Everyone has turned ugly and nasty and I can't stand it."

"I'll talk with her," Jenny promised. Just stay out of her way for the rest of the day, and I will make it right."

"Please!" said Maya, and she left Jenny's office in a rush.

"Wow," Lori exclaimed. "I don't think I have ever seen Maya with as much as a ruffled feather before this!"

"I know," Jenny responded. "Things must be more stressful than I thought! It will all blow over soon." Under her breath she added "I hope!"

The next few days as the remainder of the Atlantic Utilities order was being shipped out everyone kept their heads down and stayed out of each other's way, but things didn't get better, in fact, they proceeded to get much worse.

At 9 the morning after the last shipment, Raj exploded.

"Do you KNOW what Maya did?" He yelled at Jenny. "I had a request from Brigham International for an SKP. They are building a 150-villa resort in Tennessee and wanted me to overnight them an SKP so they could see if it would save them some money. If they found that it would, they wanted 150 of them right away, and then wanted 500 a year for the next four years. That is

One Million Dollars! So I packaged up one of our test units to ship to him overnight, and Maya repackaged it for ground! It didn't get there in time, and Brigham called and told me to forget about it!"

Jenny was stunned, until she remembered that Maya had told her that Val demanded that she reduce her shipping costs. Just as she was about to offer Raj an explanation for Maya's actions, Olga came storming in.

"You will never guess who I just got off the phone with!" Without waiting for anyone to guess, she continued, "Bill St. Clair, at Atlantic Utilities. He wants us to delay shipment of sixty of the units until he can clear out the first twenty. Of course they are already gone! Can we get the freight company to hold them somewhere until Atlantic is ready?"

Jenny held up her hand. "Lori," she called out, "Please ask the department heads to meet in the cafeteria in ten minutes. You two go walk it off, and meet us in the cafeteria." As they left, she picked up the pencil she had put in her desk drawer, and looked at it. "Communicate Intelligence," she said, as she felt like going for a long walk herself.

Chapter 21

When everyone had gathered in the cafeteria, Jenny stared at the wall. She hadn't been in the cafeteria for nearly three weeks, so the changes in the mural were a surprise.

Color had been added between the black lines. There were many different colors, and the overall picture was looking much more like the flower Maya had predicted, but the strangest flower Jenny had ever seen. Every petal was a different color, starting with bright yellow and going through all the primary and secondary colors until there were twenty differently colored petals. She was beginning to think that she had the answers to what it was going to end up being, and who was responsible.

Ignoring that for the moment, she turned to the group.

"You have all been working unbelievably hard, as have your people, and I want you to know that I think you are doing a terrific job, but I also know that it has been a tremendous challenge, and we have not been doing a great job of communicating with each other. It doesn't really surprise me that a few days ago I got a pencil that said "Communicate Intelligence."

"We have missed the boat on this one lately, and I hold myself responsible since I cancelled the morning meeting thinking that it would give you more time to handle all of the rush work you have taken on. Obviously that was a huge mistake, and I hope that I won't find myself pressured to make that mistake again.

"Additionally, we haven't done a good job of communicating outside of the organization either. Olga just told me that Atlantic Utilities wants to delay the delivery of the Mega units which are, of course, already on their way. Perhaps we should have asked them to check their storage capacity when they placed the order to ensure that they would be prepared for them. We might have had a bit more breathing room on the production end if we had known that we could slow the process down.

"We over extended ourselves financially as well, and unfortunately that has resulted in the loss of a potential order of $1 million over the next four years for the SKP.

"I am not going to point any fingers, because when I point one at you, there are four pointing right back at me, so I want to affirm that I am asking us all to do a better job of thinking through all the questions we need to ask, all the commitments we have made, and how they impact each other as well as our customers and suppliers.

"Ultimately, we have to have our own act together to provide the right products and the right services at the right time to the right place. We haven't done that very well.

"Please, if you feel overwhelmed, talk it out with someone either here or at home, and try to reduce the damage that acting rashly might bring with it. It isn't just about lost orders and lost money, but it is also about hurt feelings and disappointment.

"If we want to build networks with our customers and our suppliers, and if we want to operate as though we are all a part of the same team, we have to start right here, with those of us here at this table.

"You are a strong team, and you have proven yourselves capable of so much more than I ever thought you would be called upon to do, and I want you to know how proud I am of you. The Lightning Bolt Company is in wonderful hands, and I know we will continue to be successful in spite of the occasional lessons that come along.

"Thanks for all you do. Now, Val, please talk to the freight company about storing the sixty units that are already on their way to Atlantic. Olga, please work with Atlantic and then with Val on a delivery schedule. Raj, talk to Brigham about another chance for the SKP, and Maya, please check with the department head requesting shipment before you take it on yourself to change shipping instructions.

"I am most heartily sorry for my own contribution to the chaos. Please try to have a better day."

Chapter 22

Jenny was convinced that the spy in her organization knew everything that was going on in the company, and was subtly directing the leadership of the organization by leaving hints at the right time in the right place. It was somewhat unsettling and a little scary that someone had that much knowledge about the company. Whoever he or she was, and Jenny thought she knew, apparently had psychic powers of observation and a very subtle way of communicating messages using colored pencils.

After the crisis of the past few weeks she wasn't really surprised to walk into her office and find a pencil that said "Align Goals." She realized that the members of her executive team had been focused on their individual departmental functions to the detriment of the success of the company as a whole.

Olga was focused on selling as much as she could even if it stressed Brian's department. Val was consumed with keeping lots of money in the bank just in case it was needed, even if it meant missing opportunities for more business. Raj just wanted to design new products and bring them to market, and Brian just wanted to make his production numbers, meet the unit cost goals, and meet delivery commitments.

Jenny was focused on ensuring that the company survived and with luck thrived, and she thought that this was really the most important goal of all.

She knew that many businesses were overseen by a Board of Directors, and that a Board might require that the CEO present a plan for major capital expenditures, potential sales revenue, total expenses, and projected profit by year for the next so many years. Jenny knew that in publicly traded companies every investor was looking to maximize their return on investment, and if they found a new way to invest money with a higher projected return they would switch their investments.

It was much easier in a family-run business. As long as the family thought that the business made sense, they would continue to invest even if they weren't getting a huge return.

The Lightning Bolt Company had never had a real business plan. Her grandfather had started the company on the basis of an idea that became successful. The company grew by word of mouth as customers talked about how good the products were, and orders just kept coming in with very little effort required in the sales or marketing area.

It was different world today. Customers were more demanding, suppliers wanted more stability, and her staff wanted to know the future.

She decided to set up a series of one-on-one meetings to get ideas from each member of her executive team.

Her first meeting was scheduled with Val, who was one of those people who would often take work home, work on weekends, and who generally did _far_ more than most people did during a normal eight-hour shift.

Val opened her tablet and proceeded to show Jenny the Excel spreadsheets that contained the best information she could put together for the financial forecasts for the next five years. It didn't take long before Jenny lost focus. There was just so much data, and a lot of the information seemed irrelevant. Something was missing, and it bothered Jenny. "Where are the assumptions on which these forecasts are based?" she asked.

Val replied "I projected from the previous sales history and extrapolated the trends over the next five years."

"Olga might know something coming up that you need to include," Jenny gently pushed.

Val was one of the smartest people that Jenny had ever met, and it didn't take her long to get Jenny's point that financial planning was a team activity.

Jenny suddenly realized that her own approach was wrong. She had been planning to collect the input from each of her senior leadership team and then put together the overall plan. She now realized that this was exactly the wrong thing to do. She couldn't align goals that were in fundamental conflict.

If she asked Brian to cut the amount of money he spent in purchasing, he might be tempted to buy in larger quantities so that he could take advantage of price discounts for large orders. If she asked him to get the lowest unit cost in production he would be tempted to make larger quantities of products to build for inventory so he could take advantage of lower production costs. Every decision they made had the potential to become a trade-off between two different departments. This was not aligning goals.

Jenny suggested they meet as a team, and asked Lori together everyone together.

When they met, Jenny showed them the pencil, and talked about her conversation with Val. She suggested that they work together on a business plan, using everyone's input on what the company did well, what the company did badly, what their skills and core competencies were, and where they needed to invest to strengthen the organization.

She shared that she thought that they could benefit from each other's experience and that the end result would be a plan they could all buy into, as they had all been involved in its development.

She asked everyone to clear their desks and be prepared to participate in a business planning workshop the following Monday to establish a company business plan for the next five years that would be based on their combined input. The end result would be a plan that Jenny would expect them all to sign in red ink.

By Monday morning Jenny and Lori had turned Jenny's office into a conference room, moving the desk out, and a table and chairs in. Easel boards and white boards, sticky notes, notebooks, pens and pencils were piled up in the center of the room and sodas, coffee, muffins and fruit were on a table by Lori's desk.

When everyone had filled up their coffee cups, she said "I'd like you to think about what the Lightning Bolt Company will look like twenty years from now. What will it feel like to work here? How many people will there be? What will everyone be doing? What will we be making? What will our facilities look like? What will our campus look like? Then take the sticky notes and write those things down, one on each note, and post them on the wall. When you have all of your thoughts down and on the wall, we will move on to the next step."

Thirty minutes later nearly 100 notes on the wall in different colors of paper, in no particular order.

"Great work, everyone," she said. "Together these notes represent our view of the future; what we think that we will be doing in twenty years. Together they represent our vision, which is the first step in the process of developing a coherent plan for the company. If we can agree on a vision, then we can plan how to achieve it.

"The next step is to form our vision statements into groupings that you think make sense. Quietly, without talking to each other, move the notes around so that they seem to fit with the other notes around them."

When the work was done, and all the groups had been formed, Jenny said "Now let's look at each group and write a statement that reflects what the notes in that group convey, and then we pool all those statements together, and that becomes our vision."

When they were done, their vision was "The Lightning Bolt Company, empowering the world with intelligent power networks," and when they continued the process they determined that their mission was to "to bring intelligent control of power to everyone."

"Now," Jenny said, "each of you should develop your own department goals so that they support the mission. Once that is done, you should develop your action plans accordingly and we should all be working toward the same thing.

"It will mean that as we come together as a group and need to make compromises and decisions, we can ask ourselves 'how will each choice help or hinder performing our mission?'

"All of our goals and actions should then be aligned with the mission.

"Does that make sense?" she asked.

"Absolutely," said Olga. "It means that we need to find the things that prevent us from making every power system we can and eliminate those things so that we can deliver the system to everyone who wants one."

Val added, "And we should try to make it as inexpensive as possible so that we truly can provide them to everyone."

135

"I think we need to look hard at our plant layout now that we will be making two different systems, and redesign the layout to facilitate the mission," Tim added.

Brian nodded.

"I think it all works," Maya said, "and I think it will help us focus when we get overwhelmed."

"Great," Jenny said. "I think this was a good use of our time. Let's spend the rest of our time together defining and refining some of our departmental goals and seeing how they come together."

Chapter 23

When the group next gathered for their daily meeting, a new colored pencil was sitting on the table. This one simply said "Deliver Solutions."

Whoever was leading this game knew enough to get them thinking. Maya was the first to speak. "I think that the person who is giving us these pencils is a follower of Socrates. He was a great believer in getting people to learn for themselves by asking them questions and then letting them discover the answers by themselves."

Raj replied "That would never work today. Socrates could ask the students questions all day long, and they would just go to Google for the answers!"

Jenny asked, "So what does it mean 'Deliver Solutions'?"

Olga said, "The best products are the ones that fill an unmet need and solve problems. We are in the business of creating solutions to real problems that real people have. Any problem in the world can be treated as a business opportunity. It's all about seeing what needs to exist and then making it.

"Look at all the products that you thought would never be needed and how big a part of our lives they are now. Why would anyone buy water in bottles, when it is delivered to their homes in a pipeline? What about the company that is literally selling fresh air in bottles to people who live in areas with high levels of air pollution?"

"What about pet rocks?" Jenny asked. "I know they were successful, but I fail to see the problem that they were solving!"

Tim had an answer. "They didn't succeed, really. They were a fad. I think what we need to focus on is real problems, real needs."

Now it was Val's turn. "We all know about a company that was in the business of making typewriters. Then they started making business machines, and now they are in the solutions business. The company has evolved and morphed into a different entity over the past century. Most of their sales revenue is not generated by selling hardware, but by their consulting business selling solutions to business problems."

Jenny said "We need to adapt as well, so let's brainstorm some ideas about how we can deliver solutions. Why don't we start with listing our own problems? Take a few minutes and write down your five biggest problem areas, and please, don't put another person's name on any list. Let's avoid personality conflicts and focus on the process issues that need to be addressed."

Silence prevailed as the team members started to compile their lists. Jenny watched with pride as she saw how the group was coming together in a way that had not been their normal practice. She knew that habits could be created by repeating processes a few times until it became a standard routine, and the daily meeting now fell into a good business practice that had become a new way of life for her company.

People seemed to get a lot out of the meetings and they had definitely created a much calmer atmosphere. People looked happier.

She remembered meeting a man from a company whose business card read "Vice President of Fun and Human Resources." It was a cool concept, so she asked him how he measured "Fun" and he replied "I measure smiles per hour!"

She looked around the room and didn't see many smiles, so maybe she had some work to do to improve her fun metric, but at least the people weren't yelling at each other.

After a few minutes she asked them to share their problems, and it was amazing how many people had identified the same problems. Lori facilitated collecting the problems and created a file that she projected on a wall. It was surprising how many times the same problem had been raised. As a result they were able to create a list of the top five problems facing the company. It was a valuable exercise.

The number one problem that the team had identified was "Fire fighting or expediting."

This was inherent in their business. They reacted to crises as they occurred. The Atlantic Utilities problem was just the most recent example of how they conducted business. Things went wrong, people dropped everything to fix the problem, and they never knew when the next crisis would happen.

Jenny didn't know how to fix that. It seemed the normal way of doing business. It was the exact opposite of delivering solutions.

She knew that some businesses just seemed to run very smoothly. She was really impressed by a tour she had taken of one company that was still making the same products it had made for the last fifty years. Each single unit fit with every other unit that they had ever produced. They never seemed to have problems like defective materials, mistakes in the process, or people messing up, yet her company was constantly plagued by problems.

She now realized that she didn't have to do everything on her own; that she now had a great team to help her, so she gave them a challenge. "Think outside your own functional area. The only way we can solve a system problem is to have a comprehensive and cross functional approach."

Jenny had always worked in traditional pyramid organizations where top management made all the decisions. These were then communicated down the organization through successive layers of middle management until finally they reached the people at the lowest level in the organization who performed the work. Information very rarely flowed back up the organization, and if it did it was doctored to reflect what the bosses wanted to hear, rather than the actual truth. There was an established chain of command, and everyone knew where they fit into the pyramid structure.

Jenny addressed her executive team. "We need to find a way to change our normal business practice of reacting to crises as they occur. What practical steps can we take now, that will put us in a stronger position so that we are in command of our own destiny, instead of responding to crises. What can we do to prevent the crises in the first place?

"I want you all to think about solutions from a company perspective, not just what other people can do to help you. That is the old way. Now you have to come up with companywide initiatives that will make a permanent difference. You have one week to come up with some solutions, individually or together as you want. I look forward to hearing your ideas next Monday. I know we are heading in the right direction. Let me know if you need any help."

The group stood and moved to go back to their departments, talking excitedly as they went. This new process of short daily meetings was really helping to build teamwork, and it looked to Jenny like the group felt that she was supporting them. Overall the atmosphere in the company was much more positive since the mysterious pencils had started arriving.

Chapter 24

Dave knew the value of people, after all that was his profession, but he had a hard time convincing Val that people actually had value. She was an accountant and to her people were a payroll expense. The more people on the payroll the more it cost the company. He had tried to explain that they were an asset but to no avail. To a finance person, people could be depersonalized to 'headcount'. The fewer heads the better.

It reminded Dave of the term used in his profession by recruiting firms who often called themselves 'head hunters.' It conjured up unpleasant memories from when he had visited the museum in Suva on vacation in Fiji and he had seen the cannibal cutlery that the islanders had once used when they were dining on the first unlucky tourists to visit the islands.

Dave had received a colored pencil today and it made him think about the way the Lightning Bolt Company treated people at work.

The pencil said "Develop People."

"Easier said than done," he thought to himself. "I have been trying to do that for years."

He disliked the name of his profession, 'Human resources.' It implied that people were a commodity that could be bought, sold or traded on an exchange like slaves. He knew, however, exactly how he wanted to address the topic of developing people with the management team at the daily meeting.

He greeted the others in the cafeteria and showed them the "Develop People" pencil that he had received that morning.

Jenny asked him to explain what he thought it meant, so Dave explained that he saw people as an asset, with varying degrees of value. He was well aware that companies often talked about their people as blue collar workers if they worked on the shop floor and white collar workers if they worked in the office, and he had even heard of the newer term gold collar worker, meaning someone who had so much value to the company that they were worth their weight in gold.

Dave described his visit to a Korean company that really did consider its people as assets in the true financial sense. This company had created a capital account for each of its people. They measured the amount of money that they had invested in their Human Capital and showed the combined value of their workforce on the balance sheet. This combined workforce asset value was adjusted each year based on whether the person had gone up or down in value. They allocated an amount each year for the depreciation of their human assets over their expected useful working life, and this annual budget amount was used to fund ongoing education and training programs to help their people appreciate in value. They had set up their own university to teach subjects useful to their people and this was fully funded from the depreciation account.

They discovered that people actually appreciated the education in new ideas and training in new tools and that they became much more valuable to the company. It truly was a win-win situation, and Dave thought that this was a great way to develop people.

Val said "We can't do that in this country. We operate under generally accepted accounting principles that tell us where we can account for costs. According to these principles people are a period expense, and we can't put them on the balance sheet with an asset value. You can't inventory people and reconcile some value to some book value."

Jenny stepped in to support Dave's point of view

"You know, Val, we often put intangible assets on our balance sheets. One example is the patent for the

Mega system. In fact we put a value on the patent, but it is extremely hard to quantify."

Val was silent.

Dave continued. "In my experience this company was an exception. I know that most companies consider their people as an expense, and there is usually no time and very little money set aside for people development. In fact the opposite is true in most companies. They are trying to save money by outsourcing jobs to lower wage areas, reducing payroll expenses and using temporary workers to avoid paying benefits. Education and training are normally the first place management looks to make budget cuts when the business needs to save money.

"The prevailing management philosophy in most businesses appears to be that workforce education and training are luxuries that companies can easily manage without. I have often heard it said 'If you think education is expensive, try ignorance!'

"Too many companies try to hire at the lowest end of the food chain, but this creates a false economy. Often when you seek the lowest payroll cost you end up paying more in terms of mistakes, lower quality, less productivity, more defective products, process errors, and shipping mix ups. When a company suffers these kinds of business losses they have usually compounded the problem by hiring more people as supervisors and inspectors to police the work of the others."

He continued, "I know of one insurance company that has committed their people to be in training programs one day in every three. That is a huge commitment to training but it pays off because they are continually assessed as having the best insurance agents in the business."

Dave had obviously given it a lot of thought.

Olga agreed with him. "Yes, I have seen companies where people work hard but not very smart. People always work smarter when they use the right tool for a job, but the key is to know which tool is required for which job. Look at what has happened to us! We have become more valuable to the company because of what we have learned from the Pencil Czar!"

Everyone laughed.

When the laughter ended, Val asked "What happens after you have spent all that money training those people and then they quit?"

Dave replied "Would that be worse than not training them and having them stay?"

Jenny realized that it was up to her to bring the group back together. "Let's think about what kind of education and training we need to develop our people. Do we need to job share and get people cross-functionally trained? Should we have mentoring programs? What kind of professional certification programs should we offer? Should we do more on the job training? What are your thoughts?"

"That is a lot to choose from," Maya replied. "Maybe we should review what we need in our own areas and get back to you with some specific recommendations."

"Yes," Jenny agreed, "but I would also like to consider what kind of cross-functional business process education and training programs would be helpful, for example to support the introduction of our new product. Please consider this as a part of your recommendations."

Everyone agreed and the meeting came to a close.

Chapter 25

Tim knew it was only a question of time before he would become the recipient of one of the colored pencils that were changing the company. He had spent some time thinking about the likely coded message that might be sent his way and he imagined it would be something vaguely related to his work in facilities. He wasn't far wrong. Two words on the pencil delivered to him were "Maintain Assets."

Now he was forced to think about the nature of the assets that he was responsible for. First were the buildings. Second, he was responsible for the equipment installed in each building. Third was the parking lot and lawn and garden area. Fourth were the people who reported to him. These were all assets and all had to be maintained.

He was glad his pencil didn't say resources. He was in Dave's camp when it came to dealing with people as assets not expenses. Tim had some very qualified people, in fact the most talented mechanics were the ones that could work on any piece of equipment and know instinctively how the equipment could be fixed when it didn't work. He had identified various skill levels that he required. At the lowest level he had hired people who had the right attitude. These were his entry level mechanics. They required a lot of close supervision, as they learned from his more senior mechanics. As time progressed the junior people would move through the ranks from novice or entry level, though junior mechanic to senior mechanic to master mechanic, and the best would make it to Master Craftsman.

Tim never rose above master mechanic, but he considered himself fully qualified to be the departmental manager. He had identified all the maintenance tasks that needed to be done on a regular basis and qualified his people for each task depending on the skill level. He continually held training sessions, and had created a color-coded spreadsheet which showed all his mechanics across the top and all the tasks on the rows. This way he could identify on the spreadsheet which mechanic was qualified to do which task by way of a simple color coded cell. A green cell indicated that the mechanic was qualified to perform the task; a yellow cell indicated they could do it under strict supervision as they learned the job, and a red cell indicated that the mechanic was not qualified to perform the task.

He also made sure that they kept up with the licensing credentials they needed in each of their areas of specialization.

He was also well aware of the capabilities of each of the building systems and production machines that were in his area of management. He realized that the bigger the building, the more complex the systems became. The building itself was around 300,000 square feet and had a single level for the production space and two floors in front for the offices. He had just finished reconfiguring the heating and ventilation systems to accommodate the new extraction fans he had installed on the roof.

He knew that the best way to maintain buildings and equipment was to perform regular scheduled maintenance. He had been on several cruises and was impressed by the way the crew was constantly performing maintenance activities. Whenever the ship was in port for a day, the crew was painting the outside of the ship. When the ship was underway they had back-up diesel engines that could be overhauled while the ship was in motion. The crew was always doing cleaning, housekeeping, and maintenance activities that enabled the ship to keep sailing, and the only time it needed to go into dry dock was once every five years.

He wanted to adopt this model for the building and all its systems. The only problem he had was persuading Brian to give up some production time on the equipment so that he could perform the necessary preventive maintenance that would make the equipment perform better in the long run. It was a constant battle to get the equipment for routine maintenance. He knew that Brian was measured on equipment utilization, and every time he handed over the equipment to Tim, his productivity measures dropped, even though the maintenance was absolutely necessary.

Tim had suggested to Brian that there were some ways he could reduce the amount of downtime on the equipment. One of these was to get the production workers to do the routine cleaning and simple maintenance activities on every shift. Another was to find ways to reduce the amount of time it took to set up each run on each piece of equipment. Brian was interested in both of these potential ideas. In particular, he wanted to gain the extra capacity that was now being wasted by having excess times for changeovers.

Tim had agreed to use a digital camera to record a video of a typical set up on a Computer Numerical Control (CNC) machine, and he then played the video for the machine operators and challenged them to see if they could come up with ideas that would cut the set-up time. They had done this fairly easily, and in fact reduced the set-up time from ten minutes to two minutes.

Tim had then offered to help Brian set up flow racks in production that were gravity fed. This way parts could be delivered to the production operators in the most effective way, arriving at the right height to enable economy of motion so that this reduced unnecessary time and reduced injury as well. Tim had shown Brian and the production people a video from a car company that had a cycle time in each work cell of 68 seconds. It was amazing to think that every step in the production process had been broken down into simple elements that could be performed within the 68 seconds before the car went to the next station down the line.

This was exactly the kind of high volume production process that would be necessary for the new SKP product that would require the ability to change over very quickly from one type of unit to another. The challenge here would be to produce these units in a flow process that was both fast and flexible.

At the next team meeting he and Brian shared the floor as they explained what they were doing to "Maintain Assets" and challenged others to think about their own assets and how they might improve the ways they maintained them.

153

Chapter 26

Jenny looked at the mural on the wall, which was nearing completion. She had suspected for a while that the painter knew far more than he let on, and she felt it was time to confront him with her suspicions that he was the mysterious guide who had been planting the seeds for the success of their business through the vehicle of the colored pencils.

She went to Paul's storeroom, where she found him repairing a floor buffer, and she asked him to join her in the cafeteria.

When they arrived in the cafeteria she pointed to the mural on the wall and asked him when it was going to be finished.

Paul replied, "It is taking shape nicely but it isn't quite done."

Jenny gave him a knowing look. "Paul, what are you doing?" she asked.

"My job is to keep the place spick and span, and when I came here I saw all kinds of things that needed to be tidied up, so I have just been doing my job."

"You have done a great job," Jenny said. "The place looks wonderful and you have really improved things around here, but something tells me you are not just cleaning the floors and painting the walls."

"Well, perhaps not," Paul said, "but I did tell you that if you didn't like it you could paint over it."

Jenny replied, "I am not talking about the mural, Paul. I just hadn't realized that your job included distributing pencils and guiding our business."

"Well," Paul said, "my old company gave me a set of those pencils when I left, and I thought that you might need them. I am just doing what I can to help your company succeed. After all, it is in my best interest if I want to keep my job."

"Thank you," Jenny said. "Look Paul, I know you are not a janitor, so what on earth are you doing here? You could be a very successful business consultant."

"Well, your dad asked me to keep an eye on you."

"What?" exclaimed Jenny.

"Your dad and I were good friends," Paul said. "We met in college, and did an internship together before he met your mom. I went on to start my own company and he went on to work in his dad's. We didn't see each other often, but we kept in touch. We shared what we learned with each other, and over the years we developed some ideas that we were going to put in a book, but he died before we could do it. I am so very sorry for your loss."

Jenny's grief at her father's death suddenly returned, and she turned away from Paul in order to pull herself together.

When she had composed herself, she asked Paul "Why didn't my dad tell me these things that you learned?"

Paul replied, "He intended to, Jenny. He was so proud of you and was so pleased that you were interested in the business. He just didn't have the time to implement them or to teach them to you before he died. Everything always happens much more quickly than you think it will, and finding the time to both implement and teach just wasn't possible while still running the company. I continued to work on our ideas, and to be honest, I wasn't all that successful implementing them at my own company.

"I had a board of directors that was only interested in quarterly results, and I was told to maximize profit. I had to cut costs all the time, run the business by budgets and returns to the shareholders. I hated it, so when they made me an offer to leave, I accepted it and retired.

"My wife and I moved to the area, but frankly I was bored to tears, and I kept thinking that if I had it to do over again I would focus on those things that were important.

"I came up with 20 basic principles that I am sharing with you."

"So we still have some more pencils to come?" asked Jenny.

"Yes," said Paul, and he took a pencil out of his pocket. "Here is the next one!" and he gave it to her.

She took it and read the inscription which said "Earn Loyalty."

"What does this mean?" she asked.

"You seemed to be doing a pretty good job of figuring it out as a team," Paul replied. "Why don't you take this pencil to your morning meeting?"

"Thanks again," she said. She was grateful to have found the source of the guidance they had been receiving, but she wasn't sure she wanted to go public with the truth: that they were being led by the janitor.

She shared the latest pencil with the group. "The Pencil Czar struck again," she grinned and she opened

158

the meeting by asking what they thought "Earn Loyalty" meant.

Olga was the first to reply. "It means that you behave in a way that engenders loyalty in others so that they make a commitment to you. It is a bit like getting to know someone, learning to trust them, and then deciding to be faithful and loyal to each other for the rest of your lives."

"Good thoughts," Jenny said.

Brian was next. "I think it means being loyal to a group, like your family, and then earning their loyalty in return. That way you will be with each other and support each other through whatever challenges you both face in life."

"Great," Jenny responded.

Maya spoke up. "I think you are both talking about a personal commitment, and that's great, but what we would like is for our customers to make a lifelong commitment to us. We would like to have lifelong customers who are so loyal that they would never even consider going with a competitor."

"Excellent," Jenny replied. "Now how can we earn that kind of loyalty from our customers?"

"Well, I know a company that has the most loyal customers in the world," Dave said.

They were all intrigued and were anxious to hear what he had to say next.

"The company is Harley Davidson, and their customers are so loyal they have the company logo tattooed on their skin!"

Everyone laughed. "I am not sure that I would want our customers to go quite that far," Jenny said.

"How did Harley Davidson earn that loyalty?" she asked the group.

"They have such a strong following because it is considered to be a 'lifestyle choice.' It is about being rebellious and living the American Dream. Harley is selling an image, and they make more money on their accessories than they do with their core business," Dave explained.

"Should we try and emulate them?" Jenny asked.

Maya replied, "No, that is not what our customers want. I would rather emulate Apple. The Apple logo has value and their customers are also amazingly loyal."

"So how did Apple earn the loyalty of their customers?" Jenny asked.

Maya answered "Well, they did a great job of being first to market with brand new products that the world didn't even know they needed. Now, everybody wants their own iphone, ipod, ipad or i-anything. Word of mouth is what sold the products, and we can do the same thing. We can sell an SKP to every home on the planet if we are first to market, if the product is designed really well, and if it performs really well. Our customers will be loyal, and we can get the lion's share of the market before the competition even realizes what is happening."

"Great idea," Jenny said. "How about gathering testimonials from our first users talking about the benefits they have experienced by using the SKP? Do we have a way to collect this information on our website?"

"Not yet," Val responded, "but I will talk to our website developer and ask them to include this."

"Great meeting," Jenny said. "Now let's get on with having a great day!"

162

Chapter 27

The team was feeling quite satisfied that they were achieving great results in every area of operations. Their customers were happy, their employees seemed happy, they themselves were certainly happier, yet the mural wasn't finished. They now felt quite certain that the mural portrayed the many colored pencils that they had already received, and they could count that there were twenty in total. As of this point they had received sixteen of them, and they couldn't imagine what challenges the last four were going to represent. They only knew that they would ultimately make them a better company. They had trust in the process, even though only Jenny knew who the Pencil Czar was.

Jenny, by this time, had experienced the change that the pencils had brought about, and trusted the process. She had talked with Paul about his wisdom, and had refrained from asking him what messages the last four pencils would offer. It was hard, on the one hand, to know that they still had so much work ahead of them, but at the same time she knew that they were reaching the end of their journey and would be a much better company for it. She was already thinking about the kind of celebration she would host when the mural, and the journey, were finished.

She was initially surprised, however, by the next message: "Sustain Community," until she realized that up until now they had simply been dealing with internal processes, customers, and suppliers. She could see clearly that everything that they did inside the company had an impact on the community outside their own four walls.

She decided to challenge her team to come up with some ways in which they influenced the external world, and to come up with some ideas about how they could do more.

At the next morning meeting she showed the pencil to her team and gave them the challenge.

"I want you to think about some of the ways that we influence the external community right here, within 20 miles of us, and how we influence the entire state and even the entire country. I think that once we have a list of some of these ways we impact the world we might have some ideas about how we can do better."

Her team accepted the challenge, and within a week she had received a fairly comprehensive list that when tabulated looked like this:

1.   Our personnel policies directly influence the families of our workforce which then influence

their spending, their health, their satisfaction, their enthusiasm and in turn their work.

2. Our waste, whether time, money, scrap or trash is not just a waste to us, but it is a waste to the community, the state and the earth.

3. The community has needs we have the resources to meet, and we should be doing more to improve the community within which we live and operate.

4. Our people have talents we are unable to make use of in their day-to-day work, but we might be able to use to improve our community.

5. The UN Global Compact lists ten goals, and we should be evaluating ourselves against each of them on an ongoing basis, in particular promoting greater environmental responsibility, not just ourselves, but in our suppliers and our customers.

Jenny was inspired by what her people had suggested as ways in which they could work to better sustain the community around them and vowed to recruit people from among their own workers to explore ideas for these important challenges.

Chapter 28

When Jenny arrived ten minutes early for the morning meeting, she found yet another pencil on the table. This pencil said "Measure Results."

She had been thinking about this for quite a while. At school she had taken science classes and she had been taught to present information in a very structured way. She was a big fan of the scientific method; she liked to experiment and knew how to present everything as if it were a science project. She liked the methodology of stating the purpose of the experiment, describing the testing method, collecting the data, documenting observations, presenting results, and forming conclusions.

It was rare to find such a systematic approach here at work.

Those who led the Lightning Bolt Company were submerged in daily, weekly, and monthly reports and Jenny was sure that over 90% of the data contained in the reports was practically useless.

She knew that Val collected and prepared detailed financial reports of every single general ledger account code. Most of this was completely useless historical information about costs versus budgets. These reports showed positive or negative variances based on actual versus planned cost expenditures, and Jenny had no practical use for this information. The budget was simply a financial forecast based on a set of assumptions that may or may not be valid.

The customers didn't care about the Lightning Bolt Company's budgets, costs, or variances. The only thing the customer cared about was the selling price of the product, and this could be expressed in terms of value.

Jenny believed in the concept of delivering value to customers rather than measuring the cost of operations. She liked the concept of costing at an automobile manufacturer where they didn't care about the individual cost of each car produced, but simply took the total cost of running the operation on an hourly basis and divided it by the number of cars produced in the hour. This gave them the average cost per car. That was good enough.

Based on this result they could figure out how much profit they were making every hour and this very important number was the essence of their business model.

Jenny was convinced that if the products were flowing to customers on a regular basis then profits would be flowing into the company at the same rate.

The bottom line was not how much profit was being made, but the rate at which profit was being generated. This was her most important performance indicator. She even had a new term for this it was called "Profit Velocity."

She had visited other companies and had seen the way information could be presented in the form of a business dashboard. She liked the idea of Key Performance Indicators being displayed and had even designed an ideal "Management Dashboard." It would have only five displays, each recording real time information, but storing the information in a history file and tracking cumulative numbers within defined reporting periods.

The information she wanted was: Sales Volume, Profit Velocity, Perfect Order %, Customer Satisfaction Survey Results, and Employee Satisfaction Survey Results.

At the next meeting she talked with the team to discover what they believed to be their most important measures, and they agreed that each of them would work with Val to develop a display board for their own departments that could easily demonstrate how well they were doing. A side effect would be that Jenny's display would hang in the lobby so that customers and employees could see what the executive team thought was important.

Chapter 29

Paul came into Jenny's office and handed her a pencil. It said "Reward Performance."

He turned to leave.

"Wait a minute, Paul. Let's talk about this," Jenny exclaimed.

"Why?" Paul asked. "You never needed my help before."

"Well, seeing as you are already here, please tell me what is wrong with the way we reward performance in this company."

"OK," Paul said. "You asked for it!"

"You have two systems in play here; one for the important people, you know, the ones who can park in the reserved spots in front of the building, and another for the less important people who come in the back door. Do you think that is fair?"

"Well," Jenny replied. "The people in the offices are making decisions that determine the company success in the long term."

"Yes," Paul countered. "But do you add value? Do you think that your customer would be happy knowing how much of the price tag for their SKP goes directly into the pockets of you and your executive team?"

"You are criticizing your boss," Jenny said.

"You asked for it," Paul replied. "I was all set to leave."

"OK," Jenny relented. "What else do you see?"

"Well, in my company we did performance reviews on all our employees once a year. I had 100 people in my operations group, and basically I had two weeks to complete 100 reviews. It was a monumental waste of my time, and it didn't do anyone any good. I was tempted to go to a website that claimed to automatically generate performance reviews using a standard boilerplate with sections where all you needed to do was write the adjectives."

"Well," Jenny replied. "How else are we going to do reviews of our people?" Jenny asked.

"The problem is that people need much more timely and more personalized feedback on their performance than on an annual basis. If someone does an excellent job they shouldn't have to wait a year to hear about it. They should be told immediately. People need to be thanked with true sincerity as soon as possible after the deed is done.

"Motivation is not something that can be imposed or demanded, but it comes from within. The most motivated person in the world is a committed volunteer. They love what they are doing so much that they do it for free.

"I often saw people de-motivated because their boss looked over their shoulder, correcting what they did, and criticizing their performance. That doesn't bring out the best in people.

"Once one of the administrative assistants in my old company saw a quarterly bonus check made out to her boss. It was roughly ten times her annual salary. Needless to say that did not help her motivation."

"So we should change our performance appraisal system?" Jenny asked.

"Only if you want to change people's behavior," Paul replied.

"People should get what they deserve. If the company does well, everyone should share the benefits. If the company does badly, everyone should share the losses.

"Make everyone a participant in your bonus system. Check out the remarkable results of the Semco company in Brazil. The CEO, Ricardo Semler set up a profit sharing scheme where everyone in the company participated in a bonus plan that distributed 22% of their net profit back to all their employees."

"I have never heard of Ricardo Semler or Semco," Jenny said.

"Well, they have been one of the most consistently successful companies in Brazilian history. Ricardo Semler wrote about the way he conducted business in a book called *The Maverick* in which he described his radically different approach to business. It is very similar to the Richard Branson story. He was a guy with virtually no formal business education, creating successful companies by thinking differently about the way they do business."

Clearly Paul was in his element, and he continued.

"I remember one of our suppliers had a problem with their union, which was being obstructive. I suggested that they try a carrot approach instead of using a stick. Their previous method had been 'the floggings will continue until morale improves.' They asked me what I meant, and I told them to find out what people wanted and do it. It turned out that most of the people in the company were working mothers who were often late for work because they were dropping their children off at day care. The children didn't want to go,

174

and would cling to their parents and cry as the parent tried to leave for work.

"The solution was simple. The company hired a team of qualified day care people and set up their own day care facility at work. They offered it as a benefit to the parents who worked there.

They used the atrium of the building, which had a mezzanine floor, and they installed one way mirrored glass, so the parents could look in on their children during breaks and make sure they were playing nicely, while the children just saw a reflection of happy children playing together. The parents weren't gone as long, could have lunch with their children, and were immediately available in the event they were needed. It did wonders for employee morale and company productivity. The union decertified itself after 25 years because management had become 'too nice.'"

"Well," Jenny said. "You have given me lots to think about. I think I need to go talk to my team."

At the team meeting everyone agreed that they needed to ask people what would improve their excitement and enthusiasm about their work, and they agreed to program a profit-sharing plan in the budget.

Chapter 30

Jenny knew that everyone was watching the countdown as the final pencils made their way into the meetings. Whether they were found on the table in the cafeteria or on the desks of individual department heads, they had become integral to the success of the business, and they all knew from the mural that one last pencil was due.

Paul had continued the colorful mural, which clearly had twenty colored pencils in a circle, with their points facing the center. The team believed that Jenny had simply provided Paul the idea and the pencils, even though she had said nothing about it. They assumed that he was developing the mural after the pencils arrived, not before. Had they thought about it they would have realized that the shape of the mural had taken place before they had received more than just a few of the pencils, and that the mural clearly defined twenty pencils long before the last one was due.

Jenny didn't care. She knew that the "lessons" were ending and that the team was truly remarkable in how well they had mastered Paul's principles.

Jenny had asked Paul to let her know when the last pencil was going to be delivered so that she could plan a celebration. He agreed, and had told her on Monday that on Friday morning he would deliver the last pencil.

Jenny talked with Lori, and together they planned a celebratory lunch for Friday noon, with a half day off for everyone following the celebration. Jenny had another plan, as well. She was going to reveal the Pencil Czar and his history to the team.

Sure enough, as they gathered around the table on Friday morning they saw the final pencil which held the message "Integrate Everything."

"What is left to integrate?" Brian moaned. "We already have networks with our suppliers and our customers. We all have our dashboards up so that our people can see how we are doing. We are active in the community in ways we never thought we would be, and we recycle darn near everything!"

"I think that we have done a remarkable job," Jenny replied. "In fact, I think all we have left to do is to make sure that we are using every means at our disposal to ensure that we continue to do those things as well as any other things that will help us keep focused, keep communication lines open, and keep everyone on the same page. I think that our Business Plan, our departmental meetings, our Sales and Operations Planning meetings, our special Community Action

Teams, and even the mural on the wall will help keep us fully integrated in everything we do.

"Can any of you think of anything else we can do to integrate everything?" she asked.

"I have been thinking of implementing cross-functional teams in production," Brian offered. "I think that if everyone understood everyone else's job, there might be more cooperation and less conflict."

Maya asked "What if once every couple of months we got all of our people, all 100 of them, together in the cafeteria at the same time and had presentations of awards, recognition for things really well done, and a pep-talk or group training?"

"That would be cool," Olga said. "We could even bring in a customer or a supplier once in a while to talk about how their business fits in with our business."

Tim had an idea too. "We could start a company newsletter that everyone could take home. That way our families could learn more about what goes on here every day."

"Yes," Dave cheerfully added. "And we could have an open house once a year and invite the community in to see our operation. We might be able to recruit some good talent that way."

Val, not to be outdone, said "I think we need to write a book about our journey."

Everyone turned to her in shock. "Why would anyone care?" asked Maya.

Val answered, "I think that our story is incredible, and I think that we have not only a story to tell, but lessons to share on what makes good businesses great."

Jenny felt like jumping for joy. She was so incredibly proud of how far they had come, how much they had learned, and how well they worked together as a team that she truly felt that the celebration she and Lori had planned was the perfect culmination to the journey.

"Let's get all of those ideas on an action list, Lori," Jenny said. "And finally, I would like to invite you all to a special celebratory lunch at noon, for everyone, right here in the cafeteria, and I have a story of my own to tell you. Thank you all," she said. "See you at noon."

Chapter 31

People started arriving at about 11:45, and lunch was waiting for them. They began serving themselves, and when everyone was seated and enjoying their lunch, Jenny stood up behind a podium that had been brought in for the event.

"Thank you all for agreeing to put aside the lunches you brought from home," she said, and everyone laughed.

"I know that most of you have not been directly involved in making the decisions that we have been making over the last few months to improve everything that we do here at the Lightning Bolt Company, but I am sure that you have felt the impact.

"We have a significantly better way of doing business, of communicating with our suppliers and our customers, and are even rolling out a plan to get money directly to you if we do well as a company."

There were cheers all around.

"I thought you might like that," she responded.

"What none of you know is who is behind the 'magic' that has happened here."

She motioned for Paul to come stand beside her.

"Many years ago, my father had a good friend, and together they worked to develop some principles that would help good businesses become great. My dad never had a chance to share them with me, but fortunately his good friend did.

"Paul applied to work here as a janitor, partly because he was bored in retirement, but also because he had promised my dad to watch out for us.

"He shared his principles with the executive team through the use of colored pencils with the principles etched on them, and continued the lessons for everyone with this fantastic mural." Jenny indicated the mural on the wall, which was now complete, with a globe centered in the circle created by the pencil points. Twenty pencils, each a different color, and each with a different principle on it, made a beautiful circle within the rectangular mural, and the globe conveyed the idea that the world depended on these principles.

"I don't know if Paul will stay with us, now that we exemplify the principles he has taught us, but if he does, it won't be as the janitor."

Spontaneous applause broke out in the crowd, and Paul, his skin slightly reddened at the attention, simply lowered his head in acknowledgment.

"In recognition of Paul's incredible contribution to this company, I am initiating the 'Paul Jenkins Award'. This award will be given any time and every time that someone deserves it for making a significant contribution to the Lightning Bolt Company, and I would like to ask Paul to come up here and help me present the first two awards."

Paul came to the podium, and taking a note card from his pocket, he read:

"For his incredible development of the 'SmartKiloPower' system, the very first Paul Jenkins Award goes to Raj Singh."

Raj looked totally shocked, and it wasn't until his coworkers pushed him up to the stage that he started to move. He took the trophy that Jenny handed him, said "Thank you so much," and returned to his seat.

Paul continued. "The second award goes to Brian Vizir, for streamlining the production process and getting the very first SKP units out the door at the same time he met the Atlantic Utility order for eighty 'SmartMegaPower' systems.

Brian was both shocked and speechless as he came up to the podium to claim his trophy.

Jenny continued. "We haven't forgotten any of you, nor all the work you have done as well. There will be an extra 5 percent in your next paycheck, and you all have the rest of the day off. Eat your lunch, and go back to your work centers, turn off your computers and your machines, and enjoy your weekend."

More cheers greeted this announcement, and Jenny walked to each of her department heads, shook their hands, and said a heartfelt "Thank you."

Appendix A

The Mural

For a full color electronic version of this artwork,

Email ClaireVBloom@gmail.com!

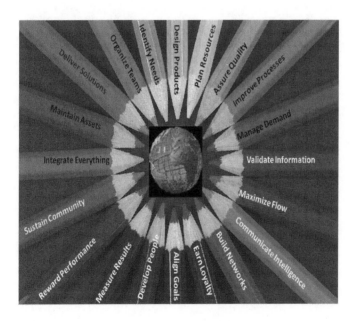

b

Appendix B

Chapter Matrix

Business Process or Function	Principle	Chapter
Coming together as a team	Organize Teams	Chapter 5
Identifying demand	Identify Needs	Chapter 6
Designing products and services	Design Products	Chapter 8
Planning and inventory control	Plan Resources	Chapter 10
Quality management and control	Assure Quality	Chapter 12
Process improvement	Improve Processes	Chapter 13
Demand management	Manage Demand	Chapter 14
Information management	Validate Information	Chapter 16
Flow management	Maximize Flow	Chapter 18
Supply chain management	Build Networks	Chapter 19
Communications management	Communicate Intelligence	Chapter 20
Business planning	Align Goals	Chapter 22
Business strategy	Deliver Solutions	Chapter 23

Education and training	Develop People	Chapter 24
Facilities management	Maintain Assets	Chapter 25
Financial management	Measure Results	Chapter 26
Reward and recognition	Reward Performance	Chapter 27
Customer relationship management	Earn Loyalty	Chapter 28
Corporate social responsibility	Sustain Community	Chapter 29
Integrated enterprise management	Integrate Everything	Chapter 30

d

e

f

Made in the USA
Columbia, SC
23 July 2017